JUNG

Looks for Trouble

16

JUNGLE DOCTOR
Looks for Trouble

Paul White

CF4·K

10 9 8 7 6 5 4 3 2 1

Jungle Doctor to the Rescue ISBN 978-1-84550-499-1

© Copyright 1953 Paul White

First published 1953

Reprinted 1954, 1956, 1958, 1961, 1963, 1965

Paperback edition 1972

Published in 2009 by Christian Focus Publications, Geanies House,
Fearn, Tain, Ross-shire, IV20 1TW, Scotland, U.K.

Fact files: © Copyright Christian Focus Publications

Paul White Productions,

4/1-5 Busaco Road, Marsfield, NSW 2122, Australia

Cover design: Daniel van Straaten

Cover illustration: Craig Howarth

Interior illustrations: Graham Wade

Printed and bound in Denmark by Norhaven A/S

Since the Jungle Doctor books were first published there have been a number of Jungle Doctors working in Mvumi Hospital, Tanzania, East Africa - some Australian, some British, a West Indian and a number of East African Jungle Doctors to name but a few.

Scripture quotations taken from the HOLY BIBLE, NEW INTERNATIONAL VERSION. Copyright © 1973, 1978, 1984 by International Bible Society. Used by permission of Hodder & Stoughton Publishers.

Some Scripture quotations are based on the King James Version of the Bible.

African words are used throughout the book, but explained at least once within the text. A glossary is also included at the front of the book along with a key character index.

CONTENTS

Fact File: Paul White

Born in 1910 in Bowral, New South Wales, Australia, Paul had Africa in his blood for as long as he could remember. His father captured his imagination with stories of his experiences in the Boer War which left an indelible impression. His father died of meningitis in army camp in 1915, and he was left an only child without his father at five years of age. He inherited his father's storytelling gift along with a mischievous sense of humour.

He committed his life to Christ as a sixteen-year-old school boy and studied medicine as the next step towards missionary work in Africa. Paul and his wife, Mary, left Sydney, with their small son, David, for Tanganyika in 1938. He always thought of this as his life's work but Mary's severe illness forced their early return to Sydney in 1941. Their daughter, Rosemary, was born while they were overseas.

Within weeks of landing in Sydney Paul was invited to begin a weekly radio broadcast which spread throughout Australia as the Jungle Doctor Broadcasts - the last of these was aired in 1985. The weekly scripts for these programmes became the raw material for the Jungle Doctor hospital stories - a series of twenty books.

Paul always said he preferred life to be a 'mixed grill' and so it was: writing, working as a rheumatologist, public speaking, involvement with many Christian organisations, adapting the fable stories into multiple forms (comic books, audio cassettes, filmstrips), radio and television, and sharing his love of birds with others by producing bird song cassettes - and much more.

The books in part or whole have been translated into 107 languages.

Paul saw that although his plan to work in Africa for life was turned on its head, in God's better planning he was able to reach more people by coming home than by staying. It was a great joy to meet people over the years who told him they were on their way overseas to work in mission because of the books.

Paul's wife, Mary, died after a long illness in 1970. He married Ruth and they had the joy of working together on many new projects. He died in 1992 but the stories and fables continue to attract an enthusiastic readership of all ages.

Fact File: Tanzania

The *Jungle Doctor* books are based on Paul White's missionary experiences in Tanzania. Today many countries in Africa have gained their independence. This has resulted in a series of name changes. Tanganyika is one such country that has now changed its name to Tanzania.

The name Tanganyika is no longer used formally for the territory. Instead the name Tanganyika is used almost exclusively to mean the lake.

During World War I, what was then Tanganyika came under British military rule. On 9 December, 1961 it became independent. In 1964, it joined with the island of Zanzibar to form the United Republic of Tanganyika and Zanzibar, changed later in the year to the United Republic of Tanzania.

It is not only its name that has changed, this area of Africa has gone through many changes since the Jungle Doctor books were first written. Africa itself has changed. Many of the same diseases raise their heads, but treatments have advanced. However new diseases come to take their place and the work goes on.

Missions throughout Africa are often now run by African Christians and not solely by foreign nationals. There are still the same problems to overcome however. The message of the gospel thankfully never changes and brings hope to those who listen and obey. The Jungle Doctor books are about this work to bring health and wellbeing to Africa as well as the good news of Jesus Christ and salvation.

Fact File: Meningitis

Meningitis is inflammation of the protective membranes covering the brain and spinal cord. It may develop most prominently in response to bacteria and viruses, but also physical injury, cancer or certain drugs. It is a serious condition. The most common form is treated with antibiotics and requires close observation. A severe headache is the most common symptom followed by neck stiffness.

Fact File: Tick Fever

Tick Bite Fever is a bacterial infection transmitted by ticks. Symptoms may include fever, headache, malaise and a skin rash. Being bitten by ticks usually occurs during outdoor activities in rural or wilderness areas. The symptoms can vary considerably in severity, but can be treated with antibiotics.

Fact File: Malaria

In Africa, a child dies from malaria every thirty seconds. Malaria is an infectious disease that kills between one and three million people every year. Most of these deaths occur with young children in Sub-Saharan Africa.

When a mosquito bites, a small amount of blood is taken in which contains microscopic malaria parasites. These grow and mature in the mosquito's gut for a week or more, then travel to the salivary glands. When the mosquito next takes a blood meal, these parasites mix with the saliva and are injected into the bite.

The parasites grow and multiply in the liver and it can take as little as eight days or as long as several months before the parasites enter the red blood cells. After they mature, the infected red blood cells rupture, freeing the parasites to attack other red blood cells. Toxins released when the red cells burst cause the typical fever, chills, and flu-like malaria symptoms.

Malaria can be reduced by preventing mosquito bites with mosquito nets and insect repellents. Spraying insecticides inside houses and draining standing water where mosquitoes lay their eggs are two ways of controlling the disease.

No vaccine is currently available; preventative drugs must be taken continuously to reduce the risk of infection but these are often too expensive for people living in the third world. Malarial infections are treated through the use of drugs, such as quinine. However, drug resistance is increasingly common.

Fact File: Pneumonia

Pneumonia is inflammation of the tissues in one or both of your lungs. It's usually caused by an infection. At the end of the airways in your lungs there are clusters of tiny air sacs called alveoli.

If you have pneumonia, these tiny sacs become inflamed and fill up with fluid. As well as making you cough, the inflammation makes it harder for you to breathe. It also means your body is less able to absorb oxygen.

Pneumonia can affect people of any age. However, in some groups of people it's more common and can be more serious. For example:

- babies, young children and elderly people,
- people who smoke, and
- people with other health conditions, such as a lung condition or a lowered immune system.

People in these groups are also more likely to need treatment in hospital. Some forms of pneumonia can be more severe than others, depending on the cause. Mild pneumonia can usually be treated at home. People who are otherwise healthy usually recover well. However, complications can develop. For people with other health conditions, pneumonia can be severe and may need to be treated in hospital. Sometimes pneumonia can be fatal. It is possible to treat it with antibiotics such as penicillin.

Fact File: Words

WORDS TO ADD EXPRESSION AND EMPHASIS: Eh, Ehh, Hah, Heee-eeh, Heeh, Heh, Heya, Hoh, Kah, Kuh, Ohhh, Ooh, Ooooh, Ugh, Uh, Yah, Yoh,

TANZANIAN LANGUAGES: Swahili (main language), Chigogo or Gogo (one of the 150 tribal languages)

SENTENCES/PHRASES:

Acha - Don't do that.

Chokwiwona - We will be seeing one another.

Habari gani? - What news?

Hakali mitindo - Early in the morning.

Hodi? – May I enter?

Jambo - How are you?

Kali sani - Very fierce.

Ku mwezi - To the west.

Lete nzeg-nzeg - Bring the stretcher.

Lyaswa - The sun has set.

Magu gwe gwe - That is your affair.

Mahala matitu - Black magic.

Miti ya nhongo - Sleep medicine.

Mzuri tu - Good only.

Nhawule? - What's up?

Nili meso - My eyes are open.

Tabu sana - Great trouble.

Tula malaka - Scraping of the throat (native medicine)

Ukubita hayi? - Where are you going?

Washenzi-shenzi - Heathen ones.

Yali yatamigwe - He has sickness.

Zu wugono? - How did you sleep?

WORDS IN ALPHABETICAL ORDER

Bado - Not yet

Chewi - Leopard

Dudus – Insects/germs

Fundi - Expert

Ibululu - Courtyard

Ihoma - Pneumonia

Itumbiko - Sacrifice.

Izuguni - Mosquito

Karibu - Come in/welcome

Kaya - House

Kumbe - Behold!

Lwivi - Chameleon

Mafigo - Stones

Mbisi - Hyena

Mbuyu - Baobab tree

Mhungo - Malaria

Muganga - Witchdoctor

Ndogowe - Donkey

N'gombe - Cow

Nhunhu - Drum

Nyani - Monkey

Nzoka - Snake

Sikuku - Party/feast

Simba - Lion

Sungura - Rabbit

Tayari - Ready

Vilatu - Shoes

Waganga - Witchdoctors

Bwete - Useless

Cihulicizizo - Stethoscope

Duka - Shop

Hongo - Behold

Igwingwili - Caterpillar

Ikolongo - River

Ilimba - Musical instrument

Kanzu - Long garment

Katali - Long long ago

Kiboko - Hippopotamus

Kwaheri - Goodbye

Machisi - Evil spirits

Majifu - Salt bush

Mbukwa - Good day

Mesomapya - Grandfather

Mpala - A Buck

Ndege - Bird

N'go - No

Nhembo - Elephant

Nhwiga - Giraffe

Nzoglo - First cockcrow

Shauri - Discussion

Shaitani - The Devil

Sungala - Rock rabbit

Swanu - Good

Uze - Come

Wulipicizo - Compensation

Zimba - A Buck

Fact File: Characters

Bwana - Dr White, main character/narrator
Daudi - Hospital manager
Elisha - Carpenter
Kefa - Nurse
Ng'oma - Witchdoctor
Perisi - Wife of Simba
Sechelela - Head nurse
Suliman - Indian

Hezeroni - Postman
M'bovu - Village chief
N'yani - Cripple
Samson - Handyman
Simba - Lion hunter
Yacobo - Previous patient

1
Vicious Village

The ward door of our C.M.S. hospital in Central Tanganyika flew open.

'Bwana,' cried the tall African with a spear in his hand, 'he's stabbed! He's stabbed!'

I was listening to the chest of a small boy. The stethoscope in my ears stopped me from hearing clearly what the newcomer said. I removed the earpiece in time to hear Sechelela, the head nurse, say:

'You can't come into the ward like that. How dare you interrupt the Bwana when he is at work!'

'But,' panted the African, 'but Simba's stabbed! He's right over there.' In the high-pitched voice he indicated the direction he meant. 'Bwana, he's in the village of M'bovu. It is a matter of great danger. They think that he will die.'

'*Hongo*,' said Sechelela, 'who stabbed him?'

'Quietly, everybody,' I said. 'Kefa, go and get me the emergency surgical kit, the one that's on the second shelf of the theatre cupboard. Daudi, a sterilized syringe, and a bottle of morphia; also the bag for anaesthetics. Samson, make sure that we have the *nzeg-nzeg* – the stretcher.'

They hurried off to get the necessities for a jungle emergency. I picked up my topee and walked out of the ward.

'Sechelela, I will come back later in the day and finish this work. Give that child the medicine I have written in the book. Also …'

At that moment Perisi appeared in front of me.

'Bwana,' she cried, 'have you heard the news? They have stabbed my husband, Simba! Behold, he went over to the village of M'bovu to speak the words of God. He knew that the Chief there had no joy in hearing them. He had heard that there would be words of anger but, behold, he went, and *yah*, Bwana, they say he is stabbed and perhaps even now he lies dying in that evil place!'

I turned to the old African senior nurse and the young African wife.

'There is one most constructive thing we can do, here and now, and that is to tell God about it, to ask for His help.'

So with bent heads, on the veranda of a hospital not far from the Equator in Central Africa, we talked to God in Chigogo, the local language, and asked Him for clear minds and heads in the matters of ordinary medicine and surgery, and for the supernatural help promised to those who have become members of His family and have lived their lives on His terms.

Daudi and Kefa converged upon where we were standing, laden with the emergency equipment. Samson had the car at the gate. We jumped aboard and drove as fast as we could over the appalling road that led through a swamp, through a grove of baobab trees, through the tightly-matted thornbush jungle to a sinister village where the words '*mahala matitu*' black magic, were frequently mentioned in a whisper. Witchcraft was prevalent and its effects well known. The Chief himself would have nothing to do with the hospital on the hill, expressing his hostility by putting every sort of stumbling-block in the way of our activities and by doing insulting things in a subtle way. Until now he had stopped short of actual violence.

Involuntarily I ducked my head as we swung underneath the limb of a gaunt baobab tree, a limb that reached out at you like the hand of a skeleton. Behind that tree was a large African house which seemed to cower back in the thick thornbush. In front of it stalked ominously a vulture. Daudi felt me shudder.

'*Heh*, Bwana, this is an evil place. It is the house of the witchdoctor, Ng'oma.'

I looked back at that mud-plastered, flat-roofed house and it seemed to me that, although I could see no one, a score of eyes were looking at us. The vulture stirred uneasily and then flapped into the air, flying over us.

'*Yah*,' said Daudi, 'behold, Bwana, it flies on to the village of M'bovu, the Chief. *Heh*, it is a bird of bad things. I have fear.'

17

'There is much that happens in this village,' said Samson, 'that comes straight from the mind of *Shaitani*, the devil.'

I swung the wheel hard round, and we came through another baobab grove into the village, a village strangely silent. At this hour of the day the women normally would be preparing the midday meal. Fires were burning; there were great bowls half full of pounded grain, baskets used to separate husks from corn, great clay pots with porridge simmering in them, but the only sign of life was a mangy dog scratching itself in the shade.

I pulled up outside the Chief's house, got out and called,

'*Hodi?* May I come in?'

There was silence, eerie silence. Then from a doorway further down the building came an old man. I went over to him.

'*Mbukwa, mbukwa*. Good-day, Great One. I would have words with the Chief?'

'*Uh?*' said the old man, putting his hand to his ear in the way of deaf people.

I raised my voice. 'I would have words with the Chief.'

'*Uh?*' said the old man in a voice that could have been heard for half a mile.

Daudi roared, 'The Bwana wants to see M'bovu, the Chief. He has words to say.'

'*Ohhh*,' said the old man nodding, '*Hongo*, come with me.'

He moved off in the direction of the witchdoctor's house, shuffling slowly.

'Bwana,' Daudi spoke quickly, 'when *ndege*, the bird, wishes to draw your attention away from her nest, does she not flutter as though with a broken wing, hoping that you will follow, and behold, her nest remains safe? This is an old trick.'

I felt inclined to agree with him, all the more so when I saw the dog moving along the side of the house and taking a lively interest in a dark stain that seemed to be oozing through the mud wall. Stooping to do up my shoelace as we came level with this spot, I realized at once that the slow-moving stain was blood, and as I tied the knot a plan flashed into my mind.

'Daudi, Kefa, Samson, get back into the car smartly, be ready for anything.'

I gripped the wheel and contrived to point the back bumper bar in such a way that when suddenly and unexpectedly I took my foot off the clutch in reverse gear the car leapt back, bursting open the mud and wickerwork of the hut and tearing a great hole in the roof.

'*Yah!*' said Daudi. 'Bwana, you've . . .'

'No words, Daudi. Get into that house and help me get Simba out.'

He and Kefa leapt clear. Samson was a yard behind me. My finger on the button of an electric torch showed us the figure of a man lying huddled on the floor in the murk of that mud hut. From within the house eerily echoed the alarm signal of the local tribe. Again and again it echoed. There was the patter of bare feet and the grunt of anger as we bumped against a hard object. My torch shone on shining skin and the twinkle of the bright blade of a spear. I swung the beam of light on the tense faces of tribesmen and then up the long wall that flanked the Chief's cow-yard. The place was crammed with people. They stood there in tense silence, a silence that you could feel, a silence completely ominous. In the distance came the alarm cry again, and then a horrible chuckle that made my flesh creep.

The light of the torch was focused on the figure at my feet. It was Simba, and driven deeply into his ribs, just beneath his heart, was what looked like the snapped-off shaft of an arrow, with the whole of its head in the African hunter's chest. I bent down quickly to feel his pulse. It was beating quite strongly.

'Samson, Kefa,' I ordered, 'quickly, we must get him out of here into the car, into the hospital. Smartly now – up easy. *Lete nzeg-nzeg*. Bring the stretcher.'

I was conscious of figures moving forward in the darkness, that flickering light that might have meant anything in the way of an attack. Obviously the thing to do was to take no notice and carry on. Carefully Daudi and I lifted the wounded man to the stretcher. Through the jagged gash in the wall of the house we carried him on to the back of the car. Simba's eyes opened.

'Bwana,' he said thickly, 'Bwana, M'bovu stabbed ...' Then his eyes closed and his lips moved wordlessly.

The glare of the sunlight after the darkness of the African house almost blinded me. I groped for a loaded syringe and gave Simba injections which might well save his life.

The village came to life with angry tribesmen moving towards us. In my haste to get away, I tripped and fell. The syringe flew out of my hand and landed at the feet of the silent, hostile group that had encircled us. An African lad picked up the syringe and handed it to me when a dark hand grabbed him by the shoulder and pushed him away, and a harsh voice called, '*Acha.* Don't do that.'

I retrieved my hat, jumped into the car and blew the horn loudly. The wild-eyed Africans scurried for safety as we drove away in a cloud of dust.

'*Yah*,' came Daudi's voice, 'behold, it is surely the hand of God that we got away from that place without harm. *Kah*, I had doubts when we were there in the darkness. They could see us and we could not see them.'

The path swung in a wide semi-circle. I twisted the wheel and before us loomed the baobab tree that guarded the witchdoctor's house. Standing in the bright sunlight was Ng'oma in his full witchdoctor's rig, a vast, tufted headdress of piebald bull-skin, the leopard's teeth worn round his neck showing starkly against his dark skin. He raised his arms with the white bone disc on them, the sign of his evil profession. He moved majestically round as we passed, his hands lifted like claws.

'*Yah*,' said Daudi, 'see how he curses.'

'*Hongo*,' I said, 'and what are the curses of a witchdoctor when we have already seen the hand of God? Did we not pray and has not God already answered?'

'*Hongo*,' said Daudi, 'truly, Bwana, but we must pray very much more if Simba is to live.'

2
The Barb

'Bwana,' called Kefa from the back of the car, 'drive more gently. *Heh*, behold, the arrow is doing damage within his chest. Drive gently.'

At that moment came the ominous hiss of a puncture.

'*Hongo*,' said Samson, 'Bwana, I will mend that. You do what you can for Simba.'

We both jumped to the ground. With a speed and dexterity that spoke of long practice he unscrewed the spare wheel, got the jack into position and proceeded to remove the flat tyre.

'Bwana,' said Daudi, 'what should we do?'

'Cover the wound, prevent infection, treat for shock and put a sterile dressing over the wound.'

I washed my hands under the thin stream of water from the spout of a battered kettle which Kefa poured for me and examined Simba, cleaning as best I could the edges of the wound, and then putting a large pad over the whole area. Strips of sticking-plaster kept it in place. Gently with my finger I tapped his chest in the way that doctors do. Kefa listened attentively. On the side that was not damaged came the ordinary note of a normal chest, but on the side where the arrow lay within the actual chest, the sound was peculiar and drum-like.

'*Yah*,' said Kefa, 'Bwana, it sounds as though the chest that side is empty.'

'*Heh*, that is just it, Kefa. Behold, does not your lung collapse if a hole is made in the chest well, like the one made by this arrow? *Heh*, is it not like when a thorn is stuck into a tyre, or a nail into a football bladder? Does it not collapse? That is the reason. *Hongo*, and perhaps it is a good thing, because there will be less damage done by the rough barbs of this arrow. *Yah*, it must have gone close to his heart, though.'

My hand was on the African's pulse. It was not a particularly good pulse but it certainly showed a considerable amount of life.

'*Hongo*, things could have been a great deal worse. Come, we must get him into a comfortable position so that the arrow inside does as little damage as possible until we can remove it at the hospital.

Slowly towards us down the path came an African girl. On her forehead, above her eye, was a weird horn-like affair, three or four inches long.

'*Yoh*,' I said, 'Daudi, look at that girl. Does she not look like Chiboku, the rhinoceros, but, *heh,* the horn is in the wrong place.'

'*Kumbe*, Bwana,' replied Daudi, 'that is the work of Ng'oma. It is one of his great works as a medicine man, to remove the cause of pains in the head. He puts on that horn. There is a hole in it. He sucks all the air out and closes the hole with some juice from the rubber tree. It is left there, Bwana, for perhaps two hours and then he takes the horn off and shakes into his hand bits of bone and hair and perhaps portions of a thorn. All these, Bwana, he has in his hand already, but he says they come from within your head and they are the cause of your headaches. *Heh*, truly it is strong medicine.'

Daudi raised one eyebrow comically.

Samson got up from under the car covered with dust. He wiped the perspiration from his forehead.

'Ready, Bwana. We can move on now, the wheel is right.'

'*Yah*,' said Daudi, looking at the girl as she walked past, 'Bwana, behold, we have a greater job to do than to put a horn on a head. We must remove from within a man the barbed head of an arrow.'

Carefully I slipped the car into gear. We moved slowly over an incredibly bumpy road.

'What is it,' I asked, dodging a huge pothole, 'that is easy to get into you and is hard to get out of you?'

'Easy, Bwana. What is easier to get into you than an arrow, and what is harder to get out than an arrow with barbs on it?'

'*Heh*, and what is it that is easy to get into your soul and you cannot get out by yourself?'

'*Hongo,*' smiled Daudi, 'that is easy also. That is sin.'

'If we left that arrow in Simba's chest, what then?'

'*Kah*, Bwana, he would die.'

'Can he remove it by himself?'

'*Ng'o*, Bwana, of course he can't. It is in there very close to his heart and is very dangerous.'

I nodded. '*Heh*, we can remove it for him. It is a very good thing that Jesus can remove from our hearts that deadly thing, barbed, that would produce death.'

'*Heh*,' said Daudi, 'Bwana, I am glad that I asked Him to do that for me.'

'This makes me think of the words of God. God caused Jesus, who Himself knew nothing of sin, actually to be sin for our sakes, so that in Jesus we might be made good with the goodness of God.'

We pulled up at that moment outside the hospital. Kefa ran off to see that everything was ready in the theatre, while I watched Simba being carried through the hospital door, and being laid on the bed where some years before I had seen him lie after his thigh and his shoulder had been torn by the lion.* I thought of how a blood transfusion in those days, by an African Christian girl, had meant all the difference between life and death. I thought of how she had said to me:

'Bwana, if Jesus loved me enough to die that I might have the life that goes on and on without finish, surely I could give a pint of blood to save a man's ordinary life.'

My mind went back to the time when in this very room the hunter, Simba, who lay there now unconscious, had come back from the gates of death

---

*Read *Jungle Doctor Meets a Lion*.

to ordinary life and had discovered the way to the life that is eternal. The blood transfusion had been the picture to him of how new life came from God to man. I remembered sitting out underneath the pomegranate tree and explaining to him that Jesus was the visible way that God the invisible One could be understood.

There was something now of the same appearance about the African as he lay there: the greenish tinge in his skin, his lips parted dryly and his obvious difficulty in breathing. I looked out across the plain and away there to the north was the place where he had fought with the lion, and where the claws of the king of beasts had been strong and cruel and damaging. Then I looked across at the village of M'bovu, where there was nothing of the straightforwardness of a lion, but a sinister, furtive, danger-spot, bristling with opposition.

Kefa was at my shoulder, 'Bwana, what instruments will you want?'

Carefully I went over with him what we would need. I pointed out a syringe with a long needle.

'Bring the penicillin. Behold, in this way we will bring discomfort to the germs that are at the moment rejoicing in his chest, the *dudus* that cling to the barbs of that arrow.'

'*Hongo*,' said Kefa, 'behold, Bwana, we have this medicine of great strength, while Ng'oma over there puts the horn of a ram or a goat on the heads of people and produces things that aren't there. *Heh*, surely ours is the way of wisdom.'

'*Heh*, and ours is the way that brings life.'

Minutes later the stretcher was being carried to our jungle operating theatre. Perisi behind me spoke much more slowly than usual, hiding her emotion.

'Bwana, do you think he'll be all right?'

'*Heheeh*, I think so. While I work though, you pray. The work will not be easy, but it can be done safely, and also the germs within him which could produce death, they will be controlled with the medicine, penicillin. In this next hour, Perisi, think of the peace of God, which keeps our hearts. Ask Him to keep your heart and my hands.'

The African girl nodded, her eyes dimmed with tears as she turned away. Thirty-five minutes later I removed from between his ribs a barbed head and two inches of broken shaft of arrow. Half-an-inch further up and Simba must have died with his heart torn by this ugly weapon.

Samson's voice, deep and strong, broke the silence of the theatre.

'Bwana, do you realize he must have been stabbed from behind?'

3

Instruments Arrive

'*Hongo*,' said Daudi, 'Bwana, they play the drums of initiation at the village of M'bovu.'

We paused to listen. On the wind came the hectic throb of the drums. They rose and fell on the night air. The moon was in its first quarter and by the watery light we could see moving up the hill towards the hospital, a figure carrying something. His progress was slow because of a pronounced limp.

'*Yah*,' said Daudi, 'perhaps, Bwana, we have work coming to us.'

'*Eeh*,' I said, 'or perhaps . . .'

'Yes, I think it is Hezeroni, the mail man. Behold, *heh*, he has trouble.'

'*Yah*,' said this worthy, coming through the hospital gates and dumping down his bag of mail. 'Bwana, I have a thorn in my foot, also I have news. I sat behind a baobab tree trying to remove this thorn from my foot. I heard the words of M'bovu. He says that Simba has cast a spell against a woman of that village.'

I looked at Daudi who shrugged his shoulders. Again through the night air came the throb of drums, from that sinister village beyond the baobab trees.

The dispenser brought a dish of hot water for the mail man to bathe his foot.

'*Heh*,' he said, 'we will soak it for a while, then I will put a bandage around it. Tomorrow we will remove that thorn for you. Swallow these.' He gave him pills.

'*Hongo*,' said Hezeroni as he swallowed them, 'it is a good thing to work in the place where pain is taken away. *Kah*, this hospital is a place of much help. I remember the days when I had *ihoma*, pneumonia, and the Bwana ...'

'*Heh, heh,*' said Daudi, 'we remember those days too, but tell us, what more did you hear as you sat behind the baobab tree?'

'*Hoh, hoh,*' said Hezeroni, raising his eyebrows, 'I heard that Ng'oma, the witchdoctor, had thrown the shoes to find why it was that this woman always had headaches.'

'*Kumbe*,' said Daudi, 'I will show you how it is done, Bwana.'

He picked up the cow-hide sandals that Hezeroni had just taken off. There in the moonlight he stood on a clear patch of earth. The whole of his normal attitude was changed, and something sinister seemed to grip his upheld arm. His head was thrown back, his chin pointed to the moon and his lips moved noiselessly. Beside me Hezeroni shuffled uneasily, spilling some water from his dish.

'*Yah*,' he said, 'truly, that is exactly how it is done. Watch him. See, he speaks to *Machisi*, the spirits of

the ancestors. See, he spits on the soles of the sandals and, *heh*, Bwana, see, he throws them.'

The sandals were thrown in a peculiar way in front of him by Daudi. They fell to the ground.

'*Heh*, Great One,' said Hezeroni, taking his part in the by-play, 'and what were the words of *vilatu*, the shoes?'

'*Kah*,' said Daudi in a deep voice, 'in this work I see the hand of *muperembi*, a hunter, a man of strength.'

'*Hongo*, Great One,' cried Hezeroni, his eyes rolling, 'tell us more.'

'The shoes will tell again,' muttered Daudi, picking them up and raising them above his head, and muttering some special incantations all his own.

I nearly burst out laughing when I heard the sonorous words 'potassium permanganate – acetyl salicyclic acid' – then in a hollow voice – 'sodium bicarbonate.'

I caught the twinkle in his eye as he again threw the shoes.

'*Heh*,' came his deep voice, 'the shoes tell me this is the work of the hunter, Simba. Has not his brother's son looked with eyes of love upon this woman and has not Simba strong thoughts of opposition? Behold, is not this his way of casting a strong spell?'

Again the drums throbbed loudly in the air, and Daudi threw down the shoes in disgust. He wrinkled up his nose and spat.

'*Kah*, Bwana, that's what he did.'

'*Heh*,' said Hezeroni, with a keen, appreciative noise, 'it was as though I had been there. Still my skin tingles.'

'*Kah*,' said Daudi, 'and so when Simba went across to M'bovu's village to greet his relation, somebody went in the dark, from behind and stabbed him with an arrow.'

'*Heh*,' said Hezeroni, 'who should have seen in the darkness in a house, and is not an arrow a very strong way of killing a man and doing it with great pain?'

He unlocked the mail-bag and poured the contents in a cascade on to the floor.

'*Heh*,' he said, 'they have ill-will towards us at that village, they have no time for our medicines, they have no time for the message of Jesus.'

'Truly,' said Daudi, 'it is a place of darkness, Bwana. They prefer it that way because of their evil doings. If you keep on walking in darkness God says you're guilty. There is no place for those walking in this way in His kingdom of light.'

'*Heh*, and will you have Jesus, the Light of the World, in your life when you prefer to walk in darkness? *Kah,* Bwana, does light mix with darkness? Can darkness stand against light? *Hongo!* See how even the thickest darkness is overcome by the smallest light.' He struck a match and lighted the hurricane-lantern. The vague outlines of letters and parcels came sharply into vision.

We sat on the floor and went through the letters. One parcel looked particularly interesting. It had a red registered label on it with 'URGENT AND IMPORTANT – SURGICAL INSTRUMENT ONLY.'

'What's inside it, Bwana?' said Daudi. 'It looks interesting.'

We undid the package.

'*Kah*, here's a thing, Daudi, we've wanted for a very long time. See?'

In my hand was a minute torch, so made that you could look into ears, along a polished cone-shaped affair, and a small magnifying glass was fitted so that you could see the ear-drum.

'*Heh*,' said Daudi, peering through it. 'Bwana, here is a thing of wonder. Bwana, here again is a way of bringing light into dark places. Truly, this is the work of our hospital.'

'Daudi, get me those special forceps from the theatre, that we were sent last year, will you?'

I wriggled my fingers in a special way. Daudi grinned, nodded and ran off, returning a moment later with an intriguing instrument that went by the name 'crocodile

With best wishes from one whose intense pain was relieved by a similar surgical instrument.

forceps,' for it was so made that when you put your fingers into the hand-piece, the last half-inch of it would open and shut. I remembered a lecturer saying, 'This is an admirable contrivance for removing beans or beads or beetles from small boys' noses or ears.'

Daudi was handling it very gently, and he laughed as the instrument opened and shut. He moved his fingers.

'*Heh*,' he said, 'behold, does it not look like the mouth of *nzoka*, the snake?'

'*Kah*,' said Hezeroni, 'but see, the small teeth are like the crocodile creature that lives on the banks of the Ruaha River.'

'*Kumbe*,' grunted Daudi, 'it will be just the thing tomorrow morning, when your foot has been freed from the grime, to remove the thorn which is in it.'

At that moment a hurricane-lantern appeared at my office door. A voice said:

'Bwana, the temperature of Simba is 102.2. He breathes 32 times to the minute.'

'I'll come and see him,' I said, putting the mail in its appropriate place.

'Tomorrow morning, Hezeroni, be up here and we will fix your foot.'

'Daudi, put that instrument on the shelf in the operating theatre. It will be very useful one day.'

I went from the room to the place where Simba lay. His pulse bounded most uncomfortably. His chest moved spasmodically and he murmured in delirium.

'*Heh*,' I said to Kefa, 'this is not a good thing. Behold, I fear that damage has been done to his heart and to his lungs, and it may be that his life is in danger.'

I had an uncomfortable feeling inside me which I couldn't quite place, but which spoke of danger.

Standing in the doorway was Simba's wife.

'Bwana,' she asked, 'is he any better?'

'No, Perisi, he's not so well today.'

I went with her outside. 'I don't like things at all tonight. I have ordered an injection. He did not sleep well.'

Perisi was silent for a moment looking at the ground. She swallowed, then in a normal voice said, 'I have heard words from the village of M'bovu. It appears that the boy who picked your syringe, the Chief's own son, is one whom Simba has taken an interest in. He had him playing football with the school. The Chief had strong anger because of this, and behold, was not the boy thrashed with a hippo-hide whip for doing what he did the other day in giving you the syringe that you dropped? M'bovu swears with strong words that no one from his village shall come near the hospital for its medicines or its message. He also says, Bwana, that the spells cast on the hospital will cause Simba to go to the place of the ancestors.'

'Perisi, remember that our God is Almigthy God. This is a thing that M'bovu knows nothing about.'

4
Surgery

I was using my newly arrived instrument. An old African man was sitting before me and I peered into his ear. His mouth was wide open. Daudi came up and grinned.

'Bwana,' he said, 'as you look into his ear he feels sure that you can see even as far as his throat.'

'*Kah*,' I said, 'look into his ear. He has much wax.'

Daudi peered in. '*Heh*, Bwana, surely this is a machine of wisdom. *Hoh*, now we can know whether we have moved the wax or not. We can also tell, Bwana, if there is inflammation in the ear or – *heh*, many things. It is very good.'

Then he said, 'Bwana, may I go towards the village of M'bovu? On a hill just beyond it is a relation of my father. I have words that his eyes are bad, and our black medicine should be just the thing. May I go later in the morning and give him this medicine?'

'*Heh*, you may go, Daudi, but be careful what you do as you pass through the baobab grove. We do not want to have trouble with you as well. I would hate you to return with an arrow in your back or a spear in your leg. By the way, Simba's a bit easier this morning. His temperature is down to 100, but there is still something about him which I don't like. There is a lot of fluid in his chest which I must get away. I shall do that in the theatre this afternoon.'

As I spoke I saw an African with red mud in his hair and a spear in his hand get up and walk slowly away. He had not come for medicine. Daudi watched him leave and then drew me aside whispering, 'Bwana, that one is M'bovu's spy. *Kah*, why was he here but to hear the news of Simba?'

'*Kumbe*, he may have heard that Simba is not so well but M'bovu can't get much good out of knowing that

I'm going to make special apparatus this afternoon in the operating theatre.'

Daudi picked up his eye droppers, got on to an old bicycle and pedalled down the hill.

'Bwana,' came a voice behind me, 'may I have the blue medicine?'

'Wait,' I said, 'until it is your turn and we will see what medicine you require.'

'Bwana,' said another voice, 'it is time my wife went home. There is no one to cook my food.'

'*Kah*,' I said, 'and how long has she been here?'

'Was not her baby born yesterday?'

I answered that one with a look.

'Bwana,' said the carpenter, 'I want some two-inch nails.'

And then came Sechelala's voice. 'Where is the Bwana? We want him quickly in the place of babies.'

I ran.

The day seemed to pass at high speed and in the rush of doing things I noticed the coming and going in the hospital of some strange faces, folk who were a little furtive in their actions. Several of them seemed to be standing around doing nothing, while one peered through the window of the operating theatre. I thought nothing of it. Perhaps they were from a distance, and just interested.

In the early afternoon I went up to the theatre armed with a handful of glass rods, some rubber tubing, some corks, a roll of sticking-plaster, a bicycle pump, and a pickle bottle. I walked into the empty theatre, closed the outside doors and went into the theatre proper, shutting the fly-proof doors behind me. I put my armful of gear down on the operating table and proceeded to fit a cork into the pickle bottle. I was just in the process of boring a hole in this cork when I looked down and some feet away, with its ugly head reared up, was a cobra.

I moved across the operating theatre and through the closed fly-proof doors at speed. As the bolt shot home that kept those flimsy doors shut, I let out a sigh of relief. The snake had moved across and had reared its head up and was beating it against the wire, spitting at me. For a minute I watched and wondered what to do. Then my eyes fell on a bottle of ethyl chloride on the anaesthetic tray in front of me. I took up this bottle and as the snake spat at me I pressed down the little lever, which sent a thin stream of highly powerful anaesthetic straight on to the wire near the snake's head. This enraged the creature and it struck again and again, and then I noticed that it moved backwards somewhat.

The reek of the anaesthetic was almost overpowering. I moved up to the door and slipped the bolt and, opening the door the merest crack, I sprayed the anaesthetic straight on to the ugly head of the

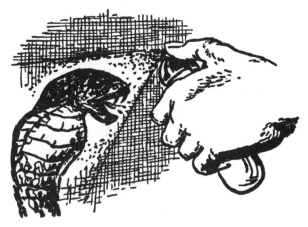

snake. For a moment it drew back and then its head swayed and went to the ground.

Now it is a principle of mine never to operate until the patient is properly under the anaesthetic and I was particularly careful on this occasion! It was only when a splutter from the bottle I held indicated that the anaesthetic was finished that I moved quickly into the operating theatre, picked up a pair of secateurs and did a neat amputation just south of the creature's head. It was one of the occasions in which the operation was highly successful, but the patient died. An idea was forming in my head and I grinned.

I took up a pair of forceps, held the snake up where I had first seen it and put the head and neck as close together as possible. Then I proceeded with my task of assembling the apparatus which was to remove the fluid from Simba's chest, and give him a very real chance of recovery. I pumped up the primus stove and sterilized this apparatus, then carrying it on a tray I went across to the ward.

'Temperature 100, Bwana,' said Kefa, 'respiration 24, pulse 120.'

'Bwana,' said Simba, trying to lift himself up on his elbow, '*yah*, it is hard for me to breathe . . .'

'*Heeh*,' I said, 'but I will take some fluid from your chest.'

Simba raised his eyebrows as he saw a pickle bottle coupled with glass and rubber and fastened to a bicycle pump, while a long needle, on another piece of rubber, led away from the bottle.

'Bwana,' he said, '*heh*, with that?'

'*Heh*,' I nodded, 'with that.'

'*Kah*,' he said, with a shadow of his usual cheerful grin, 'this is like hunting leopard in a trap with a spear. The leopard has no choice but to be stabbed.'

'*Hongo*,' I said, 'and do you give *chewi*, the leopard, a local anaesthetic before you stab him?'

Twenty minutes later it was a much more comfortable Simba who lay back on his pillow.

'*Kah*, Bwana, that feels better,' he said.

'*Hah*,' I said, 'if you have a lot of fluid inside you, *kah*, you have not room for your lung to move. Behold, Simba, there is much trouble yet. You will be lying in that bed for many days. Be very quiet.'

'Bwana,' said Simba, his voice lower than usual, 'I have been thinking. When I was in the house of my relation, just before I felt strong pain in my chest, I heard the sound of feet, but I thought it was the wife of my relation. Bwana, at the same time as that arrow was thrust into my side, my nose told me the story of an evil smell. A strange smell, such as of dying flesh, the sort of thing that happened with the man who had that very bad ulcer. And yet, Bwana, with it there was something else, something my nose never told me before.'

'*Hongo*,' I said, 'this perhaps will help us to find the person who did the damage.'

As I walked through the door, Daudi met me.

'Bwana,' he said, 'come to the theatre. I would tell you words of strong importance.'

I went into the theatre, grinning to myself as I thought of the shock that was coming to Daudi, walked through the fly-proof doors and idly picked up the crocodile forceps which now reposed in their own particular spot in the cupboard. I moved them to and fro, oiling the joints, when Daudi said:

'Bwana, there is certainly great trouble in the village of M'bovu. My relation would not allow me to give him eye medicine. He said that the Chief had forbidden anyone to taste of the medicines of the hospital. There are also, Bwana, murmurings of danger coming our way. They say that …'

He suddenly looked down and gave a yell. Grasping me by the shoulder, he almost swung me off my feet in the effort to get me out of the room.

'Bwana,' he yelled, '*nzoka*, the snake! It is behind you. See – over there!'

'Oh, that,' I said. 'Yes, the snake. I found it there earlier in the afternoon and so I cut its head off lest it should do any harm.'

'*Kah*,' said Daudi, his eyes open wide. 'You cut its head off? And, Bwana, what did the snake do?'

'Nothing. It just let me.'

Daudi shook his head. '*Kah*, Bwana, this is a strange thing.'

Then he wrinkled his nose and a slow smile came over his face. 'Bwana, you gave it anaesthetic first?'

I pointed to the spray bottle, which was empty.

'It spat at me, Daudi, so I sprayed at it, and now it's dead. Behold, I think there are many things regarding our noses which will help us in this matter.' And I told him what Simba had said.

'*Yah*,' said Daudi, 'I smelt that smell also on the man that was here at the hospital this morning. Bwana, he was near the theatre. Do you think he could have put that snake there?'

'It may be, Daudi, but he made a mistake, for no damage came to us.'

'*Hongo*,' said Daudi, 'I was reading today the words of King David. Did he not say, "The Lord is my refuge, my keeper?" Did he not say that He would protect us from lion and from snake?'

'*Heh*, Daudi,' I said, thumbing over the pages of the Bible. 'It also says about those of us who follow God, "Because he has set his love upon me, therefore I will deliver him." That's God speaking. "He shall call upon Me, and I will answer him".'

Together Daudi and I knelt down by that operating table and thanked God for being Almighty and very active on our behalf.

5
Ease of Entry

Hezeroni, the postman, was sitting on the step of the hospital, his face twisted with pain, his foot bandaged up and looking most uncomfortably swollen.

'*Hongo*, Hezeroni, you have trouble? *Heh*, did I not tell you to come yesterday that I might fix your foot? Behold, you have left it for a whole day, therefore your trouble is your own fault.'

'*Kah*, Bwana,' said Hezeroni, 'it was not that I did not wish to come yesterday, but I walked very quietly and sat behind the baobab tree where I had heard the words of Muganga, the witchdoctor. I sat there for much time, for it is a place where one is not seen and I heard words, Bwana, words that will help you. That is the reason my foot is sore. That is the reason that I have come for your help, with the sure knowledge that you will give it to me today.'

I undid the bandages and there was a foot about which Daudi, coming up, remarked:

'Behold, it looks like the foot of *kiboko*, the hippopotamus.'

'*Yah*,' said Hezeroni, 'and it throbs like the belly of a frog.'

I grinned at this elegant analogy and turned to Daudi:

'Bring the crocodile forceps, boil them up and also the pickle bottle that we used yesterday; a kettle of hot water, some antiseptic and some bandages.'

As the dispenser hurried off to do these things, Hezeroni said:

'Bwana, as I sat in the place of concealment, I heard the words of the Chief himself, and of the witchdoctor. They were concerning the girl against whom Simba is supposed to have cast a spell, the girl that you yourself saw with the witchdoctor's horn on her head. Bwana, she is dead.'

'*Yah*,' I said, jumping to my feet, 'dead? What was the cause of her death?'

I stepped back and nearly cannoned into Perisi who was behind me.

'*Yah*,' she said, 'I heard these words. Tell us, Hezeroni, what has happened?'

'Bwana,' said the mail man, 'it is a strange thing. It is beyond my understanding. Behold, the girl was eating stew made from a goat paid by the Chief to the witchdoctor, for his work in smelling out this spell Simba is supposed to have cast. *Yah*, and suddenly, as she ate, she cried out that something was in her throat, and then it was as though someone was strangling her. The witchdoctor did the work that we call *tula malaka*, but, Bwana, it had no strength to help her. For half an hour, there was much trouble and then, Bwana, she died.'

'*Kah*,' I said, 'it must have been that she swallowed a bone and it got across her larynx, the place where you talk and breathe. *Heh*, if only we'd been there!'

Daudi came up at that moment and I picked up the crocodile forceps.

'These would have been just the thing. See how you could pick up.'

I put them through the neck of the pickle bottle, and groped inside, in a way that your fingers couldn't possibly have done, and lifted out imaginary objects.

'*Heh*,' said Hezeroni, 'that would have done it, Bwana, but the fingers of the witchdoctor only pushed it in more firmly, and she died. There is great trouble in the village. Tonight you will hear the death drum. Tonight there will be great trouble all over the place.

'There will be spells, Bwana, and witchcraft and black magic. *Heh*, it is a night that makes my flesh creep, and my skin tingle.'

'*Hongo*,' said Daudi, 'you and your skin tingling. This will make it tingle.'

He had poured hot water into the pickle bottle, washed it out, and then put in hotter water. We cleaned up the place where the thorn had entered his foot, and then carefully placed the hot bottle so that the neck was directly over the hole in the foot.

'*Yah*,' said Hezeroni, full of interest, 'this is a new method.'

Then suddenly his forehead wrinkled. '*Heh*,' he cried, 'it is burning my foot!'

'Truly,' said Daudi. 'That is the way to remove the thorn.'

'*Kah*,' yelled Hezeroni, 'it will suck in my leg right up to the knee, perhaps my thigh. Bwana, it hurts! *Yah! Heeh!*'

Looking through the glass of the bottle we could see something black appearing on the skin surface.

'*Yoh*,' exclaimed Daudi, 'it will be out in a minute, that thorn. Have courage, thou that carriest the mail-bag.'

Hezeroni set his teeth and apparently was suffering agony.

'We must take that bottle off, Daudi. We're not getting the thorn out.'

I slipped the blade of a knife between the skin and the bottle neck.

'*Heh*,' groaned Hezeroni, as the pressure came down. '*Yah*, that hurt.'

'Was the thorn a straight one, or curved?'

'Bwana, it's a curved one. Were not its other relations on a stick? Did I not see them?'

I picked up the crocodile forceps, grasped the end of the thorn that was just visible, and by manipulating carefully, brought to the surface an ugly-looking, inch-and-a-half-long thorn. I put this in Hezeroni's hand. Daudi bandaged up the place where it had been, after syringing it out with peroxide.

'*Yah*,' said Hezeroni, 'it was an enemy, Bwana, that one. *Kah*, but behold, it led us to find out words that we would not have found otherwise.'

Quite a crowd of people had come around as we spoke; amongst them, one of those figures that we now had come to realize were M'bovu's men. They just came to the hospital and sat about. Apparently they did no harm but they listened, and I felt sure were up to all manner of sly tricks. I noticed Daudi slip away as I talked to the people.

'Look,' I said, 'here is a thorn. *Heh*, an ugly thorn that entered into the foot of Hezeroni here! He was walking along the path with the mail-bag over his shoulder. He did not notice it, and *yah*, in a second it was in his foot. And while it was there, Hezeroni, did it bring you joy?'

'*Kah*,' said the African, 'joy, Bwana? *Heh*, I walked only on my heel. *Yah*, it became sore, and then, Bwana, my foot swelled and all up my leg was fire. *Yah,* and it throbbed and throbbed. *Kah*, joy? While it was in my foot? *Uh,uh*.'

'It was easy to get in, however?'

He nodded. 'It was in in a second. To get in was easy.'

'Yet it was hard to get it out?'

'*Heya*, yes, Bwana,' chimed in a voice, 'there was Mpoko, of the Chimambwa tribe who died because of a thorn in his foot.'

'*Hongo*,' I said, 'it's a small thing but dangerous. Do not forget that sin is like that. Think of sin as you see thornbushes. Think of sin as you are pricked by thorns. Sin does that sort of thing. It is easy to get into you. You cannot get rid of it by yourself. Behold, all the time it is in you, it produces pain and sadness, and death. Leave sin long enough in your soul and it will certainly produce death.'

'*Heh*,' said one, 'and how, Bwana, shall we deal with this trouble?'

Then I told them about Jesus, the Son of God, and I told them that whoever believes in Him – believing means backing your thoughts with the whole of your living – has everlasting life.'

'Bwana,' said an old woman who had joined the throng, 'tell us, how did you get that thorn out of Hezeroni's foot? Did you have some piece of iron with wisdom in it?'

I took my shining forceps and showed them to her, wiggling them in the appropriate way.

'*Yah*,' they said, 'behold, this is a thing of wisdom. See how it works.'

I threw a couple of small pieces of stick into the pickle bottle.

'See if you can get those out with your fingers,' I suggested.

For a while they tried without any success. '*Yah*,' said M'bovu's messenger, 'Bwana, they will not come out.'

'*Hoh*,' I said, picking up the forceps and lifting them out in a matter of seconds.

'*Yah*,' they said, 'this is a thing of wisdom.'

'*Kah*,' said the old woman, 'it would have been good if those weapons had been in our hands when the girl swallowed the bone near the village of M'bovu yesterday.'

The African with the red mud in his hair and the spear in his hand turned on her with such an ugly look that a sudden silence came upon everybody. And then a small boy said:

'*Yah*, Bwana, behold, does not your *chuma*, your instrument – open and shut its mouth like the snake that was in the operating theatre yesterday that you killed?'

Again the man with the red mud in his hair turned upon me with an odd look in his eye. He muttered something and stalked out through the gates.

Daudi came up to me and touched me on the shoulder.

'Bwana, I have been to the operating theatre. There is nowhere that a snake could have got in. Behold, I have been trying to pull it through any hole that is available. Make no mistake. It didn't get in by itself. It was put in by one of the evil men of that evil Chief, M'bovu.'

6

The Gates of Death

'*Kah*,' said Simba, yawning as he sat up in bed. 'Bwana, I feel better today.'

That I felt was strange, in view of the face that Kefa had whispered in my ear that his temperature was 104.

'*Hongo*,' I remarked, 'can you breathe better?'

'*Heh*, I can breathe well.'

'Have you any pain in the chest?'

'There is small pain, Bwana, but small pain only, and my heart ceases to flap like a small boy beating on a drum. Nor, Bwana, does my stomach now say uncomfortable things. Nor does my interior rattle like a thunderstorm, nor yet bleat like a lonely goat.'

'*Kah*,' I said, 'what a man of words you are; stomach bleating like a lonely goat!

'Come on, lean forward. I'm going to listen to your chest with *chihulicizizo*, the stethoscope.'

I tapped the chest with my finger, starting low down and working up rib space by rib space.

'Why, Bwana,' asked Simba, 'why do you do that?'

On the ward floor was a kerosene tin, half filled with water. I went across to it, lifting it on to a stool, and then proceeded to tap my finger, moving it up the side of the kerosene tin as I had along Simba's chest. It sounded at first dull, and then came with a clear ring when my finger was above the water-level.

'*Heh*,' said Simba, 'Bwana, where there is no water the sound is very different.'

'*Heeh*, and when you tap a person's chest and the lung is solid with pneumonia you hear a dullness, but when you get up to where the lung is spongy and normal, heh, then it sounds like the note of *nhunhu*, the drum.'

'*Kah*,' said Simba, 'now I understand, Bwana.'

I put my stethoscope into my ears. 'Now, Simba, say *n'gombe*.'

He did what he was told for two minutes while I listened carefully to spot after spot over his broad chest.

As I took the stethoscope from my ears:

'*Heh*, Bwana, why do you do that? Why say the word *n'gombe*, a cow? Bwana, they would think this is a spell, the people who live in the village of M'bovu.'

'*Heh*,' I said, 'it is merely a word that echoes through your chest, like a man's voice in a big hollow tree. In my country we say *ninety-nine*, but here you have no English words, so I chose *n'gombe* as a good word. It reverberates.'

But all the time I was speaking to him I had an uncomfortable feeling inside me that something was wrong. His temperature should not be where it was and yet there was nothing to show. For four days this went on, the temperature going up and coming down. His chart looked like the teeth of a cross-cut saw, and then one morning as I made my usual examination I found underneath his knee a hard swelling. In a person with white skin it might have been visible before as a mark on the leg, but it was thoroughly camouflaged with intensely black skin, and I knew that there was a clot in one of the veins in his leg.

'*Heh*, Simba, there is trouble here. You must lie in bed very quietly. Would that I had much of the medicine, penicillin, to give to you, but we have so little in the hospital. Since we can get good results by keeping the leg very quiet, all should be well.'

'*Hongo*,' said Simba, 'this is but a small thing, Bwana, a little swelling under the knee.'

'Truly, but one small live coal from the fire can easily mean a large grass fire.'

Simba nodded.

'We must keep that leg very quiet, for if that clot were to move there would be great danger. Keep it very quiet where it is and there is no danger. *Huh*, is it not like temptation? Keep it quiet; keep it away from your life, there is no danger, but once let it move into you, and, *yah*, then there is sin. I was reading the words of Solomon. Did he not say that he who sows wickedness reaps trouble?'

'*Heh*, Bwana, the seed of the trouble under my knee, if it spreads can produce calamity?'

'*Heeh*; therefore, my friend, keep very quiet. I will paint the leg with strong medicine that smells of stale fish.'

Simba wrinkled up his nose.

'I will bandage the leg and put a splint upon it, and all will be well, but you must keep very quiet. Even now I will go and prepare this splint.'

As I went through the door I met Perisi with her baby on her back and on her head a gourd full of water.

'*Hongo*, Bwana,' she said, 'what of Simba?'

'*Kumbe*, he is not as well as I would like him to be, Perisi. In his leg, in one of the veins, is a clot. It is danger. He must be kept very quiet.'

She lowered the gourd and put it down in the shade beside the dispensary, and through the open door we could see Simba sitting up in bed.

'If he is quiet for many days, Perisi, there will be no danger, but should he get up suddenly, *yah*, there would be trouble! Therefore I will put his leg in a splint.'

'Bwana, I would greet him now,' said the African woman.

'*Heh*, greet him with many words,' I laughed, as I went off to get the plaster to make the splint.

Crouched in the shadow of a pomegranate tree was an old African with red ochre in his hair, watching an old man make string from baobab-bark fibre. Somehow he looked a stranger to me and I wondered vaguely if he were another of M'bovu's people. I collected the plaster of Paris and some old sheets of newspapers to prevent my making a mess on the floor. I walked back towards the ward and almost cannoned into Daudi.

'Bwana,' he gasped, 'quickly, quickly, there is great trouble! On of M'bovu's men put medicine in Perisi's water gourd.' The dispenser panted and continued with his story as we went at a run towards the ward.

'Simba saw him, Bwana, and had great rage because this is a thing of great evil in our tribe. He jumped out of bed, but M'bovu's man ran with the speed of *mpala*, the buck. Simba had just got through the door, Bwana, when suddenly, shrilly, came the danger signal.'

We swung round a corner to find Simba lying on his back on the ground, a crowd of people round him, Perisi bending down, holding his head up from the ground. There was a deadly tenseness about the scene. Directing matters swiftly, I had him put back to bed, his leg being held most carefully. An injection was given. Simba's skin was a weird grey-green shade.

I bent down as his lips moved. 'Bwana, I am going.'

Perisi looked across at me with agony in her eyes, and Simba said in something below a whisper – I just caught the words:

'I know Whom I have believed and am convinced that He is able to keep what I have committed unto Him for that day.'

Perisi was praying wordlessly.

At that moment the C.M.S. Sister came into the room. I looked up at her. She had sized up the situation and looked at me questioningly.

'Look after Perisi, Sister, please. Simba has had a pulmonary embolus.'

Every appropriate drug we had available came into play in that battle for life.

Four hours later, in the intense heat of the African early afternoon, the only noise being crows cawing as they flew crookedly from the baobab trees outside the hospital, I sat beside Simba's bed, my finger on his pulse. Simba's eyes flickered open.

'Bwana, the pain, the pain.'

On the hot, still air surged the sound of African singing; the tribal initiation was in full swing at M'bovu's village.

Simba listened: 'Bwana,' he said, 'they put medicine, evil stuff into Perisi's gourd and I had anger.'

Again he set his teeth and I heard the words, '*Yoh*, the pain! The stabbing with an arrow is a small thing to this pain.'

I reached for the syringe that was beside me and again injected. The crows were silent but clearly came the rhythm of the drums in the distance.

Outside the ward I heard a soft footfall. Tiptoeing outside, I found Perisi. There were deep lines of anxiety around her eyes as she looked at me, wordlessly asking the question.

'Perisi, it is very bad. Simba still stands at the very gates of death.'

7

Trouble Looms

The postman dumped his bag of mail on my doorstep.

'*Yah*, Bwana,' he said, 'there are many words on much paper within, and *yoh*, it was a work of much sweat to walk over the hills today.'

'*Hongo*, did you not stop at the village of M'bovu to hear any new words?'

'Well, Bwana,' Hezeroni smiled, 'I did stop there for a little while, and *kumbe*, I heard great news. Behold, they say that N'goma, the witchdoctor, has cooked strong medicine to produce great danger and perhaps death to Simba.'

'*Kah*,' I smiled to myself when I heard these words. '*Kah*, it wasn't his medicine. It was his messenger that produced the trouble. He came up here, and caused anger in Simba's heart when he saw him putting medicine into Perisi's water gourd. *Yoh*, but Simba leapt out of bed, forgetting his arrow stab, his leg, everything. The instinct of the hunter in him was strong, and *kah*, great damage came because of trouble within his leg. He lies there even now very close to death, although today there is a better chance of his living because he survived through the night.'

'*Hongo*,' said Hezeroni. '*Yah*, these are ill tidings.'

He shook his head while I undid the mail-bag, and then:

'Bwana, I have heard the words also there of your instrument whose mouth opens and shuts like a crocodile. This was spoken of with many words and much laughter. Muganga says it is a thing of small wisdom and of no use at all, but the man who saw it used to pull the thorn from my foot, *eheh*, he spoke words of strength. He… '

Daudi was at the door.

'Bwana, Simba's temperature is 101. He has been drinking much fluid. He says the pain is less, but he would have words with you. Also, Bwana, Perisi has not slept. She walks round like one in a dream. She sits before the food at meal-times, but does not eat.'

Hezeroni interrupted. 'Oh, Bwana, there is one more piece of news. The child of M'bovu whom Simba taught to play *mpira*, football, met me on the path beyond the place of *majifu*, the salt bush, and he asked me the words of the health of Simba. "Because," said he, "is he not my friend?"'

'*Hongo*,' said Daudi, 'you'd better come and see Simba at once. I still have very great fear, and sleep would perhaps come to Perisi if her fears, too, could be quieted.'

Gently but very thoroughly I examined Simba. There was no doubt about it, he was very greatly improved.

It gave me tremendous relief some half-an-hour later to sit beside that African girl in the shade and say, 'Perisi, the danger for the moment, anyhow, has decreased. Simba is very, very sick but he is no longer before those gates of death.'

She nodded her head, finding words too hard to say, then:

'Bwana, this has been a day of great sadness. My heart has been full of fear and my prayer has only been, "Oh, Bwana Yesu, Oh Bwana Yesu – Oh Lord Jesus, Oh Lord Jesus".'

'Perisi, He heard, He understood and He's answering. Remember, He said that we will not be tempted - that means tested any more than we are able to bear. He gives us these trials so that we can be useful to Him in a bigger way in His great plan. It's very hard for us to understand anything about it, but one day we will, mark my words. Sit quietly here. Behold, I will go and have words with Simba, then we will drink tea and you shall sleep.'

'Bwana, may I not come and have words with him, too?'

'Just a minute and I'll see.'

Simba seemed to be asleep. His eyes opened as I felt his pulse. I motioned to Perisi to come in through the door. We sat beside the bed.

'*Hongo*,' said Simba, 'Bwana, I thought I had gone on the road called 'death'. *Kumbe*, I jumped from my bed when I saw that evil man. *Heh*, I thought, would he do damage to Perisi? And then, *yah*, the pain! It was as though I had been hit with a red-hot axe, Bwana, but now it only hurts me a little to breathe.'

'Lie quiet, then, great one. Remember, sleep is your best friend.'

A look passed between husband and wife which brought a quiet smile to each face.

'Bwana,' said Perisi, 'shall we not talk to God together?'

We knelt and I thanked God for His help and asked, if it were convenient, that at a later time we might know just the reason why all this had happened.

A week later Simba sat in bed, his inflamed leg done up in plaster of Paris, propped up on two pillows which were nothing but unbleached calico stuffed with grass.

I pushed and prodded here and there.

'No pain at all,' laughed Simba. 'Bwana, when will I be able to get up?'

'You stay where you are,' I said. 'Don't you move. If the elephant put his head through the window you would stay exactly where you are.'

'*Hongo*,' said Simba, 'would I?'

'You would!'

'*Heh*,' said Simba, 'Bwana, have you seen the words of the glass nail?'

By which I knew he meant had I seen what his temperature was. I told him that for days now it had not gone above 99.

'The moon is at the full tonight, is it not, Simba?'

'*Heh*, it is, Bwana.'

'Right. Until the moon has come again to the full you will lie just where you are.'

'Bwana, what may I do? May I sing songs?'

'*Uh, uh*, you must not do anything like that, but I will give you the material and I want you to make me an instrument such as you play at night by the camp-fire.'

Simba smiled all over his face. '*Kah*, Bwana, I will have joy to make you an *ilimba*. Perhaps Elisha in his carpenter's shop may have what I require. Also, Bwana, I will want one old umbrella, some small nails, and...'

'*Heh*,' said Daudi, 'here is the one that you made for me.'

Simba took it from his hand and ran his thumb over the flattened-out umbrella spokes which were the keys. It was a peculiar sound.

'*Yah*,' said Simba, 'I have had much joy with this instrument, Bwana. Did I not make one for the son of M'bovu?'

'*Hongo*,' I said, 'I have heard that he has been sending messages to see that your health was good.'

'*Kah*,' said Simba, shaking his head, 'Bwana, that boy will have trouble if his father finds out that he is doing these things. Did not M'bovu himself have great anger? Did he not take the instrument that I made for the child? Did he not throw it on the ground and stamp upon it with his foot? Did he not curse me with many words? Did he not threaten to thrash the child if he came near me? All this, Bwana, because I told him the words of God. M'bovu is one of evil ways. He prefers to walk in darkness. Indeed his deeds are evil. Shall it be then that he will let his son find the ways of life, and hear the message of life, the life that goes on and on? *Hee*, but he's a good one that boy. Laughter comes readily to his eyes. My prayers are much for him.'

'What's his name, Simba?'

'He is called M'bangho.'

'*Heh*, Bwana,' said a voice at the door, 'I have words to tell you.'

'*Kah*,' said Daudi, 'this is Hezeroni, the postman. He has ears as long as those of *ndogowe*, the donkey.'

'*Heh*, Bwana,' said Hezeroni in high glee. 'Bwana, I have heard that M'bovu himself has a great sickness. This is a matter of rejoicing, is it not?'

'*Heh*,' I said, 'you would rejoice at his sickness? *Kumbe*, I will go and see if I can help.'

Hezeroni was immediately all concern. 'Bwana, don't go. Don't go near that village. Don't go near the place. Ng'oma is making a very strong spell and if you go there, Bwana, heh, there will be trouble. *Tabu sana,* terrible trouble.'

'Trouble or no trouble, I'm going over. The only way to help is to go God's way. He says, "Love your enemies." Also, "If a man compels you to go one mile, go with him two."'

'What does that mean, Bwana?'

'It was the custom of the rulers in Jesus' day to grab a man and make him carry loads. This was a law of the land, but he only had to go one mile. Jesus said therefore to do the hard thing, if it's going to help a man to come out of darkness into light.'

'*Hongo*,' said Simba, nodding slowly. 'I understand, but Bwana, I fear that before you lies a strange safari. In it I seem to see snakes again.' He shuddered.

'*Hongo*,' laughed Daudi, 'it sounds as though there was medicine put into Simba's water, Bwana.'

'Bwana, beware of this safari. I fear *tabu sana,* great trouble.'

8

Drums of Sacrifice

Simba sat up in bed playing tunes on his *ilimba*.

'Bwana, I have been practising with great strength. Behold, I would play you the music that I played when I carried water from the well.'

His fingers moved rapidly over the pieces of umbrella spokes, producing a not unmusical sound. I looked at his broad shoulders and thought how capable he was of carrying nearly a hundredweight of water. It would be at least a month before he would have a chance of doing that again.

He went on twanging as I examined his leg, and made sure that the plaster fitted it. I turned to him:

'Now, Simba, don't you move around. Let this plaster on your leg be as it were a bone outside your skin. Keep that leg from moving. Do not forget the words of King Solomon when he said, "A live dog is better than a dead lion."'

'*Heh*, Bwana,' said Simba, 'you think of those words also, before you go on that safari to the village of M'bovu. If you are still determined to go this way of small wisdom, then walk along the path of *ikolongo,* the river, keeping your head well down, passing through the place of thornbush; pass through the hill, *ilulu*, where I killed a leopard once, and climb the granite boulders where my tribe made their sacrifices in the days of drought. Look carefully down, Bwana. From that place you, hidden in shadow, will be able to see what is going on in the village of M'bovu. Watch carefully before you visit, for Bwana, do not forget the words of King Solomon, "A live dog is better than a dead lion".'

We both laughed.

'*Hodi*,' came a voice at the door, and I saw Hezeroni standing there, a spear in one hand, and knobbed stick in the other.

'*Heh*,' said the postman, 'Bwana, are you ready for your safari? Behold, I am ready.'

'*Heeh*,' I said, 'listen. Simba has words to tell us the path that we should travel. Listen to these words, while I get from Daudi the medicine that we might require.'

In the dispensary Daudi had packed up a canvas satchel that carried syringes, quinine, and a score of other things that might be needed, if M'bovu, the Chief, would allow me to give him medicine.

'*Heh*,' he said, 'I heard today the words that M'bovu's trouble is a very bad pain in his head, Bwana.' The dispenser laughed. 'Bwana, I have therefore put in many aspirin, but Bwana, his trouble comes from the drinking of much beer which undoubtedly has tied knots in his liver.'

I grinned at this complicated anatomical idea.

Saying *kwaheri*, I fell into step with Hezeroni and walked down the path from the hospital.

For half a mile not a word was spoken. Hezeroni swung along at a good speed, taking every piece of cover that was available. Under the shade of a great baobab tree he stopped.

'Bwana,' he said, 'listen.'

The sun beat down and there was no wind. I could hear nothing but the unlovely sound of a crow in the tree above me.

'*Uh, uh*, Hezeroni, I hear nothing.'

'*Kah,*' he said, 'your ears are blocked, Bwana. I can hear the throb of drums, and of feet dancing. Bwana, they are planning to sacrifice to the ancestors this afternoon.'

As he stood I could see his big toe moving to and fro, keeping time with a rhythm I couldn't perceive.

'I hear nothing,' I said.

'Bwana,' he said, 'I cannot hear it so much as feel it. *Huh*, you will never feel it as we do. Bwana, you will never understand as we understand.'

He was grimly serious. 'You laugh about going on today's safari. *Heh*, but I, I have great fears, Bwana. I have heard that the sickness of M'bovu is but a small thing and if we travel to his village, if we incur his anger, Bwana, then my spear and stick will have small strength to keep you safe.'

He was in deadly earnest. 'Bwana, do not go beyond the great stones where we may stand and watch it all ourselves, unseen. *Heh*, when they worship the ancestors they will have no joy in your presence. *Kah*, Bwana, I have fear. Listen to the drums. Listen to them now.'

The heat haze hung heavily but I could hear nothing.

'*Uh, uh*,' I said, 'I hear nothing.'

'*Kah*,' said he, 'my ears tell me many things but yours do not.'

Then I remembered that Daudi had said that Hezeroni had the ears of *ndogwe*, the donkey. Crouching low, we forced our way through a piece of jungle that made me screw my eyes up as we passed perilously close to great ugly-looking thorns.

'*Heh*,' said Hezeroni, 'it was here, Bwana, that I picked up my thorn. Yah.'

We had moved out into a clearing and he pulled me behind a baobab tree, with a great hole in its hollow trunk.

'*Heh*, Bwana, it is in there that many of the people of my tribe are buried. If you look in with your torch you may see their bones.'

For a minute I looked around inside that grim tree. I looked at those white skulls and wondered what story they could tell of the horrors meted out to them by N'goma, the witchdoctor, whose house I knew was not far away.

Hezeroni was peering round the edge of the tree.

'*Heh*, Bwana, this is strange. There is no one at the house of N'goma but two old men.'

I saw this native house with its pumpkins and gourds on the roof. Two old men sat in the shade playing *sola*, a game of twelve small holes and a number of little pebbles. A black-and-white goat strolled aimlessly about while an athletic little hen pecked at some grain in a crack of the sun-baked earth before the witchdoctor's house. Then on the air came the throb of drums.

'*Kah*,' said Hezeroni drawing back, 'Bwana, there is the note of the drums. This is a thing of the *washenzi-shenzi*, the heathen ones, those who have no time for God whatsoever.'

'What will they do, Hezeroni?'

'*Kah*, Bwana, many things. Among them is the killing of a black cow. This is the peace offering that they will make to the ancestors. Listen, they are singing.

'*Kah*, Bwana, they are calling on the ancestors to take strong pain from the head of M'bovu. *Heh*, Bwana, see! They have also a black sheep. *Kah*, these they will kill before the house of M'bovu for the ancestors, that they may be appeased.'

Hezeroni drew back behind the great rock where we stood.

'Bwana, is not this just what happened *katali*, long, long ago, in the days when the people of Israel killed goats? Is not this the same thing, Bwana?'

'*Uh, uh,*' I replied, 'those sacrifices amounted really to a reminder of sin. They pictured the fact that sin produces death. They were also a finger-post to point on to what you and I know, Hezeroni, but those people down there' – I pointed with my chin – 'either do not know, or will not listen to, the fact that the blood of bulls and goats and sheep cannot remove the guilt of sin. God Himself said He had no pleasure in sacrifice and burnt offerings. *Kah*, but Hezeroni, things are utterly different since Jesus lived and died, and lives again. Did not God say, in speaking of you and me and everybody else, "Their sins and their iniquities will I remember no more"? So, because of the blood of Jesus Christ, you and I, Hezeroni, may have courage to come face to face with God Himself, because of Jesus Who died and is yet alive. These are the words of God about this very matter. "In this confidence, let us hold on to the hope that we possess without the slightest hesitation, for He is utterly dependable."'

'*Yah*,' said Hezeroni, 'Bwana, those are good words. They bring real comfort. *Kah*, Bwana, but look at them.'

The drums throbbed. The wind stirred through the thornbush and I could hear clearly the words of the people some hundreds of yards away, standing outside the door of the Chief's house.

'Great One,' they chanted, 'let thy children dwell in the shadow of peace, and let them sleep in the shadow of peace.'

'Bwana,' said Hezeroni, 'beneath that doorway you see the big thornbush. There is buried the father of M'bovu and his grandfather also. Behold, Bwana, they call to whitened bones for peace. *Yah*, they might as

75

well pray to those skeletons in the tree behind us. *Heh*, surely this is a thing of small wisdom.'

And then to underline this, the drums swelled up in a hectic, fanatical beat.

9
M'bangho

Hezeroni and I crouched behind a great granite boulder. We were invisible where we sat in the shadow. Before us, a couple of hundred yards away, in the clear light of the late African afternoon, with a faint wind bringing us the sound, we watched M'bovu, the Chief, with his tribal elders, and his son, make a peace offering to the ancestors of the tribe. There was a constant singing and chanting. The words came clearly.

'Oh, Great One, let thy children dwell in the shadow of peace, and let them sleep in the shadow of peace.'

Over and over again it rang out, and then suddenly, starkly came silence. The Chief himself carried a gourd.

'*Yah*,' said Hezeroni, 'Bwana, in that gourd is beer. He will pour it over the resting-place of the great ones. Watch, Bwana, and see his son. He drives forward the black cow, and the black sheep. See, they stand before the grave of his ancestors. See, M'bovu kills the cow!'

With the swift movement of the sharp knife, M'bovu cut the throat of the black cow and the knife was passed to his son who drew back as his father motioned to him to do a similar thing to the sheep.

N'goma suddenly leapt forward, knocking the knife from the boy's hand and crying '*igwingwili*.'

This I knew referred to a sort of caterpillar.

'*Yoh*,' breathed Hezeroni, 'that is the messenger of the ancestors appearing there! It shows their ill-will to M'bangho.'

The boy hung back and clearly came some words of M'bovu:

'The ancestors have anger in your presence.'

The boy was pushed aside and the Chief himself slaughtered the black sheep. A deal of butchery went on which I regarded as neither skilled nor elegant. Portions of the anatomy of both cow and sheep were thrown on the grave of the ancestors. Over all of this further beer was poured.

'*Yah*,' said Hezeroni, 'that is the task of the Chief's son, but see, Bwana. His father has anger towards him. He does it himself. *Yah*, there will be trouble in store for Simba's friend, M'bangho. See, Bwana, how the youths of the village look at him with suspicion. They will expect the anger of the gods to be upon him. *Heh*, he is the one who will be Chief when his father dies. His father hates him but no other living boy has been born into his house.' Hezeroni pointed with his chin. 'See, Bwana, they cut pieces of meat and throw them to the north, to the south, to the east, and to the west, and above and below, that there may be no place where the ancestors are not provided with food, and *heh*, Bwana, see ... '

The Chief took from a man behind him a branch of thornbush. This he put over the offering in a tense silence. Again he uttered the words:

'Great Ones, let thy children dwell in the shadow of peace. Grant this, O Mazengo, my great-grandfather. Grant this, O *mesomapya*, my father's father. Grant this, O Malondo, my father.'

The drums throbbed, and the people suddenly let out a trill of rejoicing. A fire was lighted in a deep trench. The meat was cut up and a feast was prepared. Women came with gourds and kerosene-tins full of beer. The people crowded round to dance. It was noticeable that the Chief's son walked downcast towards his father's hut, the people standing away as he walked.

'*Yah*,' said Hezeroni, 'see him, Bwana, he has great shame. If anything happens to him, without doubt, they will say it is the anger of the ancestors.' He shrugged his shoulders.

We looked down and saw people moving across towards the witchdoctor's house which was even closer to us. Hezeroni drew me back closer to the rock.

'Bwana, we still cannot be seen. Heh, this is the place where our eyes and ears can be opened and our bodies melt into the stones beside us, even as does *sungula*, the rock rabbit, and *lwivi*, the chameleon. *Heh*, Bwana, see, they go to the house of M'bovu.'

I started forward. 'Look, Hezeroni!'

His hand was on my shoulder. 'Bwana, do not move like that. Keep quiet. We must not be seen.'

'But look,' I said, 'there is a snake! It moves towards the doorway of the house of the *muganga*. Heh, surely they will kill it.'

'*Uh, uh*,' said Hezeroni, shaking his head, 'Bwana, watch. This is a thing that no one from your country is likely ever to see again. See, they have noticed it! Heh, watch N'goma, Bwana.'

The old man, with incredible speed, moved into the house and came back with a long paddle-like affair that native women use for stirring porridge. In his hand was a gourd

containing native butter. Another African had come to the house. He moved to and fro with a weird swaying movement on the ball of his foot, playing an *ilimba*. The sound of it came vaguely up to us.

The snake swayed to and fro as though calmed by the music. It did not strike or move as the *muganga* spread native butter in thick, greasy drops over its back. Then in a sing-song voice he greeted it:

'*Mbukwa*,' and in the native language, 'We know, Great One, that you are a god come to visit us.'

'*Kah*, Hezeroni,' I whispered, 'will not the snake suddenly strike at them?'

I clutched at my bag that contained the various medicines that I had with me, feeling that any moment I would be called into action.

'*Ng'o, ng'o*, Bwana,' said Hezeroni, 'that snake is not fierce. If you treat it gently and play it music all is well, but if you do not treat it well, Bwana, *uh, uh*, it can be *kali sani*, very fierce. See, Bwana, they hasten to kill a black lamb!'

Once again I saw a piece of rough butchery performed, the skin literally torn off the lamb. N'goma came close to the snake. He covered it with the lambskin. The *ilimba* player brought more and more out of his instrument, his thumb moving rapidly over the umbrella-rimmed keys. The singing of the people grew louder and louder. The sun was setting in a brilliant colour over the hill. There was a shout of triumph from M'bovu and those around him in the dance.

'*Heh*,' they cried, 'the gods have come! Has not *nzoka*, the snake god, visited us, and taken our sacrifices?'

'*Heh*,' grunted Hezeroni in deep disgust as we crept down the side of the sloping granite. 'It is a thing of small wisdom to have confidence in a snake, and to take notice of the actions of a caterpillar.'

In the half-light of dusk we crept along the dangerous path through thornbush, and found our way into the river-bed, walking along the dry sand. Suddenly, behind us and very near, came the eerie cry of a hyena. Hezeroni gripped his spear tightly.

'*Yah*, Bwana, *heh*, it is a noise of no joy that *mbisi* makes. Let us move with speed.'

We came out of the river-bed and in the darkness came on to the usual path. As we made our way back up the hill, we could see the lights of the hospital, friendly, beckoning.

'*Heh*,' said Hezeroni, 'it is good to look up at those lights, Bwana, and to know that they mean home.'

Against the night sky I could see my companion nodding his head, while in the background came strongly on the evening breeze the rhythm of the drums.

Suddenly out of the deep shadow a shaggy head appeared and two long arms came out at Hezeroni. He drew back his spear. I grabbed his arm as a deep voice said:

'*Heh*, it is only I, *N'yani*, the monkey.'

10
N'yani - The Monkey

I switched on my small torch and there on the path was a pathetic figure. From his waist up, a man of splendid development, but his legs were mere sticks – wasted things, unspeakably crippled.

'*Yah*,' said Hezeroni, '*heh*, I had fear when I saw you there. I thought, '*Koh*, it is *chewi*, the leopard.''

'*Kah*,' laughed the cripple, 'it is only I, N'yani, whom people call the monkey. Do I not walk with hands? Do I not walk at night to avoid the laughter of those who walk on feet?'

I shone the torch down and I could see the pads made from

old pieces of motor tyre which he wore on his twisted knees, and on his hands. He moved forward with us, going at a surprising rate.

'Bwana,' he said, 'I saw a child who was blind. I saw him walk past my house. Did I not watch through the cracks in the wall? Do I not see many things? *Heh*, do not my ears hear many things? You sit in the dark, Bwana. You be such as I am and you too would watch and listen. It is my life.'

'*Heh*,' said Hezeroni, 'and, Bwana, I have heard the words that there is nobody in all our tribe who has greater skill in the making of mats than N'yani here.'

'*Kah*,' said the cripple, 'Bwana, I can make mats with my eyes shut. My hands know the way, but, Bwana, I have come to your hospital, for I thought that if you could cure a child's eye, it might be that you could give strength to a man's legs.'

'*Heh*,' I said, 'surely we will try. We will see what can be done for you. Behold, we will have N'yani, the monkey, in the bed next door to Simba, the lion!'

Hezeroni chuckled.

'Bwana,' said N'yani, 'I have come because the Chief has said that nobody from our village shall visit the hospital. Is not N'goma the witchdoctor of our village? Shall we not go to him?'

N'yani stopped. I could hear him spit in the darkness.

'I have had charms around my waist; I have swallowed charms; there were charms in my ears; there were charms around my ankles. *Kah*, Bwana, no strength has come to my legs, nor any strength to my limbs. Nor does the pain up my back grow any less. *Yah*, Bwana, so when the Chief made this order saying no one shall go, I said to myself, "I will go." He chuckled. 'I needed something like that to stir my anger, to make me make up my mind, and, Bwana, I have come.'

He went through the gates of the hospital in time to hear Simba active on his *ilimba*. N'yani crouched in a corner while a hurricane-lantern was brought for me to make an examination. From the room next door suddenly came singing. As they swung into the chorus, N'yani slowly translated the Swahili back into Chigogo.

His strong hand reached out and touched me on the knee.

'Bwana,' he said, '*heh*, it has a sound of joy about it. They are not the words that I hear round the fire in our village. I heard a song the other night, Bwana, which told of the things which you do in the hospital. How you cut out people's eyes, make them into medicine, and then put the eyes back. How you have a strong medicine that keeps people from screaming when their pain is very great. How you have medicines that turn people's insides to water.'

'*Heh*,' I said, 'those are songs written by N'goma, or by M'bovu himself. They have no joy in our work here, for there is no profit in charms that do not work when we have the medicines that take away pain.'

'*Heh*,' said N'yani, 'those are words of truth, Bwana, but can you take away my pain?'

Daudi arrived with a lantern.

'*Yah*, Bwana, I am glad that you have come back from that village. Did you give M'bovu any medicine?'

'*Uh, uh*,' I shook my head, '*uh, uh*. He was making *itumbiko*, a sacrifice. We merely watched, but we have brought one from that village whom we will help.'

'*Hongo*,' said Daudi, 'I have heard of N'yani. Is not he the one who knows everything that happens in the village?'

The cripple cowered back.

'Have no fear,' I said. 'Daudi is my friend and my helper. He will also be your friend and your helper.'

'Daudi, help him up on to this examination bed.'

Together we lifted him. He was covered with an irritating skin disease which he scratched incessantly. One big hand went over his shoulder, the other behind him, trying to reach the spot in the middle of his back, but there was a clear two inches that he could not reach. Daudi grinned and scratched the spot for him.

N'yani smiled. '*Yah*, truly he is a friend and helper. Does he not scratch the spot that irritates which is beyond my reach?'

They laughed. I examined his legs. Although there was quite a deal of gnarling of the joints, his nerves were entirely intact. His muscles had almost disappeared from disuse. Daudi looked over my shoulder.

'Bwana, is there anything we can do?'

'*Heh*, quite a lot. First we must get his story. Tell me, N'yani, why did your legs get like this?'

'*Kah*, Bwana, it was the days of the great rains. My wisdom went from me, and did not N'goma beat me with the glowing stick?'

I could see scars on his foot and leg. Apparently the witchdoctor, driving out the malignant spirits of the ancestors, had burnt his feet so that he had not walked. In the delirium of malaria his legs had drawn up and had stayed there. Moving round on his hands had pushed them more and more out of position until there he was, a wreck that need not have been a wreck, and a wreck that could be righted, at any rate to some degree.

Yacobo came into the ward. 'Bwana, will we put N'yani in the ward?'

'*Heh*, first of all though, he must be bathed.' N'yani drew back.

'*Uh, uh*, that is not my custom.'

'*Heh*,' said Daudi, 'it is a very comforting custom. It removes the itch, also it is a way of making your skin much more comfortable. Come, I will show you how it is done.'

He grinned at me, and I watched the khaki-clad African dispenser and that pathetic monument to the witchdoctor's art move away across the courtyard.

The next afternoon I came into the ward to do my routine round. I had a look at Simba's leg. His temperature was down. Everything seemed to be in order.

'*Heh*, Bwana,' he said, 'I have no pain.'

'*Hongo*, before long we will be able to get you up. But ... not ... before ... I ... tell ... you.'

Simba laughed. I turned to the next bed.

'*Heh*,' said a spruce-looking African, his hair duly shaved off and his scalp shining from the effects of peanut oil worked thoroughly in, 'Bwana, do you not greet me?'

'*Yah*,' I said, 'have I seen you before?'

He was dressed in a pyjama coat, somewhat worn, but still showing a nice collection of big red spots.

'Am I not N'yani? Did I not meet you?'

'*Hongo*,' I said, 'you look different already. *Heh*, behold, we should be able to give you much help. Lie there quietly and in a few days' time when we have put more strength into your body and chased out the *dudus* of malaria, then I will take you to the place of operation, and we will help your leg.'

'*Hodi*,' said a voice at the door, and girl of about fourteen came in, bringing a basket containing African porridge. This she gave to N'yani and went out.

'*Hongo*,' I said, 'one of your relations?'

'*Uh, uh*, Bwana. She is a girl from the village of M'bovu. There are those that say she is a relation of M'bovu himself. When he had great rage not long ago, and had drunk much beer, he hit her very hard on the head with his knobbed stick. Since then, Bwana, she has had fits. Her hands and her face shake like a bird in flight. There are those who have fear of her. They say she is bewitched, but, Bwana, I know better. She would sit with me while I made mats. I would tell her the stories of the tribe. *Heh*, Bwana, and she had kindness to me. "Are you not weak," she said, "from the middle down and I am weak from the middle up? Shall we not help one another?" So I taught her to make mats and she brought food to me, and *yah*, she brought me much news.'

Simba, in the next bed, was twanging away at his ilimba.

'Bwana,' he said, 'I have a new song. It is about a blind man called Bartimayo. It comes from the words of God. Let me sing it to you.'

'*Heh*,' I said, 'you may sing.'

As he finished, N'yani turned round and said, '*Yah*, these are words that I would hear.'

'*Heh*,' said Simba, 'these are the words that bring life. They have brought life to me. *Kumbe*, it is not a hard thing to tell of the things you know, and I know that

God helps me every day. Has not my life been in great danger twice, and each time has not God helped? We worship no snakes smeared with butter, nor strange insects with peculiar legs like sticks, nor calves with two heads, but we worship God. We understand Him because His Son came to earth like a man. *Heh*, it was He Who dealt with the eyes of Bartimayo. *Heh*, I will sing it for you again.'

11

The Spirits Strike

I was standing precariously on a petrol-box, screwing a hook into the rough-cut timber of the ward roof. On the floor beside me was a large pulley and some rope. I had just got that pulley into position when a small voice came from outside the door:

'*Hodi*?'

And in walked the African girl who brought N'yani his food each day.

'*Jambo*, Bwana,' she said in Swahili.

'*Jambo*,' I replied. '*Habari gani*? What news?'

Without looking up, in a flat voice she said, '*Mzuri tu.* Good only.'

She handed a gourd full of native porridge to N'yani, smiling quietly at him and walking off.

'*Heh*,' I said, 'she is one of few words.'

'*Kah, ng'o*,' said N'yani. 'Bwana, when she has news she can talk with great strength.'

'*Heh*,' said Simba, 'and talking of great strength, look at your legs these days. Behold, you can see them grow.'

'*Heeh*, since the Bwana has given me medicine, truly I have more strength in me. I can feel it.'

He looked at his pathetically twisted legs. '*Heh*, but, Bwana, they have small use.'

'*Kumbe*,' said Simba, 'and I just lie here with my legs in this plaster thing. I, too, am *bwete*, of small use. *Yah*, if I could take my spear and go to the forest and come back with meat, then I would be of use, but I lie here *bwete*.'

'*Heh*,' said Daudi, 'and swallow medicine, and talk many words.'

'*Heh*,' said I, 'and you stay there until such time as your temperature stays down all day, and you have no more clots in your legs to produce trouble in the hearts of your friends.'

Simba smiled, and I took a measuring tape from my pocket and measured N'yani's legs.

'Look, behold, they have increased in size by one inch in just over a week. This is a very good thing. See, this is how you must treat your legs. Massage them in this way.'

I took his very strong hand in mine and showed him just how to do this for himself, and then I showed how muscles might be contracted; the mere movement of them would strengthen the joints for the operation that was to come.

'*Heh*,' said N'yani, 'Bwana, if only I could *walk*, could walk with my *feet*. I do not ask to walk with speed, not to be able to leap, but oh, Bwana, to walk on one's feet!'

'*Kah*,' said Simba, 'I was reading this morning of two men, Petro and Yohanna, who followed Jesus Christ. Jesus died and they had sadness, and then they found that He was alive again, and they had joy, and then came strength through the Spirit of God, and, Bwana, these men who were frightened, *yah*, they had strength. One day they entered the large city, and there, at the gate of the temple where people worshipped God, they found a man, even as N'yani here, who spent his time begging for food and for money. Behold, he saw Petro and Yohanna, and when they stopped Petro said, '*Ucilanje*.' He thought that he would get some money, and then Petro said, 'I have no silver or gold, but I'll give you what I've got."

'*Yoh*,' said N'yani, a wistful note in his voice, 'would not that man prefer above all things that his legs might be strong, and straight, that he might walk?'

'*Heh*,' said Simba, 'that's what happened. Petro grasped him by the hand and he lifted him up and he said, "In the name of Jesus, rise up, walk" and the man did so. Everyone was amazed.'

'*Heh*,' said N'yani, 'if this could happen to me . . .'

'Behold,' I replied, 'we will work on those legs of yours. Even now your strength is greater, and when the day comes when you can smell the *miti ya nhongo*, the sleep medicine, then your legs will be straight and we will put them in a plaster like Simba's. We will teach you to use them again, and then, behold, with the help of Jesus, who helped the man in the story, you too will walk on your feet.'

The next day there was a deal of laughter when the pulley came into action for the first time. The rope was held in N'yani's hand, threaded over the pulley and into a sort of a cradle in which were his feet. He pulled with his hands and his legs went up into the air. This was done time and time again.

'*Yah*,' he said, 'Bwana, my legs seem to be straightening. *Heh*, but it hurts, it hurts. *Kah!*'

At that moment, a small voice came at the door:

'*Hodi*?'

'*Karibu*,' said Daudi.

And in came the small girl with her dish of millet porridge.

'*Habari*?' I said. 'What news?'

'*Mzuri tu.* Only good, Bwana.'

'Then the wrath of the ancestors has not been showered on M'bangho yet?'

The small girl shook her head. '*Uh, uh*, Bwana. *Bado*, not yet.'

I raised my eyebrows. She went out of the door.

'Not yet, *eh*? Then they expect something to happen?'

N'yani nodded his head vigorously. '*Heh, heh*, Bwana, that is so.'

'*Hongo*,' I smiled, 'and you, too, must expect something to happen. Tomorrow we will work. Eat and sleep tonight, for there will be no food for you in the morning. The operation will be a most unusual one. Never before in this country has it been done. It is a work of strength.'

'*Hongo*,' said Simba, 'Bwana, we have talked with God these days and asked for His help upon your hand and upon the legs of N'yani. *Kah*, this is a thing of wonder. We will await with eagerness the work that you will do.'

There was a freshness and exhilaration in that East African early morning. The sunrise made everything

colourful. Small boys drove cattle off to graze, and I walked up to the hospital. The drums started to throb for early morning prayers in the church.

Daudi was in the operating theatre. Everything was ready. I saw a stretcher with N'yani in it, coming down to the theatre. Kefa had rolls of plaster bandages and a large dish made from a kerosene tin cut in half, ready for my use. Samson had the anaesthetic machine all ready for action. I looked through the theatre window across at M'bovu's village lying there in the shade of baobab trees, and I thought of N'goma, the witchdoctor, whose charms brought little comfort and no relief, and then at our theatre with its instruments, its anaesthetics, what it meant in saving life, and quelling pain. Then we prayed before the operation started.

'Bwana,' said N'yani in a thick nervous voice. 'Bwana, I have fear of this medicine that brings sleep. *Kah!*' He shuddered.

'Have no fear, just relax. Remember that we are here to help you. Remember that the hand of God will be with my hand. Think of the man that Simba told us about who was lame and who, through the name of Jesus, got back his ability to walk. Think of these things.'

I put the mask over his face and started to pour on the anaesthetic.

'*Heh*,' he said, 'Bwana, these are things to think of. Bwana, they are things of joy to think of. Bwana, I sleep … think … of … these … things.'

And then he was under.

Much anaesthetic was given. He had to be completely relaxed. Kefa and Daudi helped me as with increasing pressure I drew his legs down, breaking those tough, cob-web-like adhesions that dragged his joints out of place. We were all pouring with perspiration when the plaster was ready to be put on.

'*Yah*,' said Daudi, 'look, Bwana. His legs no longer twist like the branches of *mbuyu*, the baobab tree. They are straight. *Kah*, Bwana, this is a thing of wonder. He will have great surprise when sleep leaves him.'

The plaster was almost from his hip to his heel, and shaped so that it could be put on and taken off.

'*Hongo*,' said Kefa, 'they look like a piece of guttering on the roof.'

'*Heh*, they do, indeed, but, behold, they fit close to his skin. This will support his legs that he may have small pain only. He may learn to move his hips, then his knees, and his ankles.'

It was in the early afternoon that I saw N'yani start to come out of his anaesthetic and it was in the late afternoon that he was conscious of his surroundings. He looked down at his legs encased in plaster. He saw the blackness of his skin against the whiteness of the plaster of Paris.

'*Yah*, Bwana,' he said, 'a thing of wonder; a thing of wonder. See where my feet are; far away from me. *Yah*, they have not been there for many harvests.'

Through the door came a small voice: '*Hodi*?'

'*Karibu*,' I replied.

In came the girl with N'yani's food.

'*Yah*,' she said looking down at his feet, 'the Bwana has worked with wisdom. *Kah*, this is a work of great wisdom. *Heh*, it dries up my words.'

'*Hongo*,' I laughed, 'and what is the news of the village of M'bovu?'

'*Eh*,' said the small girl, putting her hand to her mouth, 'Bwana, so surprised was I to see the legs of my friend that I nearly forgot. Bwana, there is trouble in the village of M'bovu. Behold, the spirits have struck.'

She shook her head and handed the porridge to N'yani.

'*Kumbe!*' I said, 'tell me. The spirits have struck – what do you mean?'

She shook her head. '*Kah*, Bwana, *heh*, they have struck and M'bangho has great trouble, *heh*, great trouble indeed. He …'

Her voice faltered and stopped. Her face became distorted, and then with a cry she fell to the ground, her whole body shaking convulsively.

12

Enter the Dudu

'*Heh*,' said Daudi, '*Kah*, they say the spirits have struck at M'bangho, and, Bwana, we have no news of what has happened. *Yah*, just as the child was going to tell us, did she not have a fit? *Kah*, Bwana, *heeh*. Could she not have waited for her fit for ten minutes to have told us the news?'

'Behold, very often it is the stress of things that makes people have fits, but anyhow, we shall get news before long when this postman of ours arrives. He has the ears of a donkey as you say, and he will have heard everything that goes on.'

'*Hongo*,' said Daudi, pointing with his chin through the gloom. 'See, Bwana, there he comes now. *Heh!* Truly he will have news. See, he walks with words spurring his feet.'

At a jog-trot Hezeroni swung up the path with the mailbag over his shoulder.

'*Heh*, Bwana,' he said as he came up the hill, '*heh*, here is the mail. *Yah*, water! I have thirst.'

He was given water to drink and with the gourd half-empty he panted out:

'*Kah*, Bwana, *heeh*, I have news.'

'*Heeh*,' said Daudi, 'we know. Trouble has come the way of M'bangho.'

'*Yah*,' said Hezeroni, 'trouble! *Eh!!* Words of truth, Bwana. And has not trouble crawled into him? *Heh!*'

'*Hongo*,' said Daudi, 'tell me more.'

Hezeroni, seeing that he had the news, squatted on the ground, relaxed.

'*Yah*,' he said, drinking the rest of the water very slowly. '*Heh*, crawled into him!'

Tantalizingly he smiled. '*Heh*, at the *itumbiko*, the offering to the ancestor, did not *igwingwili*, the caterpillar, come towards him, indicating the wrath of the ancestors? *Heh*, and as he lay in his father's house, did not the ancestors come upon him? And, Bwana, these are the words that I heard: "Truly he slept in the house of his father".'

My mind flew to a night when I had slept in an African house and I had seen the sons of the family wrap themselves in a threadbare cotton blanket and sleep on a mat on the floor, covering their heads and leaving their feet sticking out. I asked why this was done and had been told, '*Heh*, Bwana, behold, mosquitoes can do less harm to the ears of your feet.'

Hezeroni's voice broke in on my thoughts.

'As he lay, Bwana, on the cow-skin in the darkness at the hour before *nzoglo*, the first cockcrow, a *dudu*, Bwana, no doubt sent by the ancestors,' here he wriggled his eyebrow, 'crawled through his blanket. Bwana, it moved with stealth with all its six feet. It came to his face and then, seeing his ear, it crept in. In his sleep he stirred and, Bwana, the *dudu* moved swiftly into his ear, right in. Yah, he awoke with strength and fear. "*Heee-eeh, kah, eh!*" he said, and with his finger he dug at his ear, and pushed the *dudu* in further. Many were the noises of lamentation that he made.'

'*Kah*,' said Simba, 'you know, Bwana, the voice became shrill, "*yah, yah, yah, kuh, kuh, kuh!*"'

'*Heh*,' I said, 'I know. But what happened? Go on, Hezeroni.'

'*Heh*, Bwana, he then took some grass from the lining of the roof and he tried, within his ear, to remove the *dudu*. He caused himself pain, for the *dudu* clung with his feet to the very drum of the ear. *Huh*, by this time M'bovu himself was awake. Who could sleep with the noise the boy was making? And there were words, Bwana' – up went his eyebrow again – 'amongst the others of the Chief's household. Behold, the ancestors had struck. But M'bovu himself came to the boy's aid.

For a moment he thought, and then, taking his son by the ankles, he held him head downwards and shook with strength until the boy's teeth rattled in his head, but behold, the *dudu* clung tightly to his eardrum. *Yah*, and great was his sorrow. And *kumbe*, there were others of the Chief's tribe who stood around, and one had lighted a hurricane-lantern, and, Bwana, they did a thing of small wisdom.' Both of Hezeroni's eyebrows lifted an inch. 'They stood him on his feet again and M'bovu blew with strength into the opposite ear.'

'*Yah*,' said Daudi, tapping Hezeroni on the chest with his fingers, 'you say they blew in the *opposite* ear?'

'*Eeh*,' said Hezeroni, 'did they not wish to blow out the *dudu*?'

'*Kah*,' said Daudi, '*eh!*' He rolled his eyes. 'Behold, Bwana, they must join our anatomy class. *Kah!*'

'*Hongo*,' I said, 'Hezeroni, you need not tell me what happened. The *dudu* clung with strength to the boy's ear.'

'*Heh*, Bwana, and great was his sorrow. *Yah*, and then, behold, I heard the words that tomorrow …'

'That means even at this moment . . .'

'They would go to the house of N'goma. They will kill a goat, Bwana, and they will make an offering to appease the spirits.'

I raised my eyebrows and looked at Daudi. He shrugged his shoulders.

'*Huh*, Bwana, and what help will a piece of goatskin round his neck be to a dudu that crawls around in his ear?'

Simba broke in. '*Kah*, Bwana, *heh*, he is truly in trouble. *Yah*. A *dudu* in your ear. *Kah*, many days ago, *izuguni*, the mosquito, buzzed near my ear. I hit at him with my hand. *Yah*, he went within my ear. *Heh*, it seemed as though *mbisi*, the hyena was within my head. *Yah!!* But he walked with his many legs and pushed with his wings. I had thankfulness when he went out – *zzz!*

'*Hongo*, it will go badly with M'bangho. *Yah*, what shall we do, Bwana?'

'There is one thing that we can do – a thing of great strength. We can pray that God will help him.'

Very quietly in the next bed N'yani said, 'I have seen the power of God. My legs are straight. The hand of God was on the Bwana's when he worked with my leg. Will it not be upon his hand to help the boy?'

'But how?' said Simba.

'*Yah*,' said N'yani, 'shall we teach God His work?'

There was a nodding of heads, then we closed our eyes to pray, and asked God to help the lad in the village beyond the baobab trees, and to help us to find a way of helping him.

As we finished praying, we could hear the throb of drums coming from N'goma's place. Slow and ominous on the air, they had a threatening note about them.

I turned round to the men in the ward. 'Behold, God sometimes takes the anger of men and turns it to produce His own results.'

'*Heh*,' said N'yani, 'Bwana, because we talk to God and ask Him for things, will He, at the distance that we are from that village, do anything? Is His hand strong to work in that way?'

'*Heeh*, it says in the Bible, "Surely the arm of the Lord is not too short to save nor his ear too dull to hear?"'

'*Yah*,' said N'yani, pulling gently on his pulley and watching his plaster-covered legs going up and down, 'I will understand these words, Bwana, when I see them work out. *Heh*, the boy is in trouble, great trouble. The father is a man of power. Is it likely that he who hates the way of the hospital here will come for help to those whom he hates? *Kah*, how should this be?'

'*Hongo*, N'yani, we talk of God as being Almighty. You shall see His hand.'

'*Kumbe*,' said Simba, 'there is a song that tells us these words. It speaks of the Holy Spirit of God. Heh, shall I sing it?'

'*Heh*,' I nodded, 'sing.'

As he sang, N'yani was busily at work with his pulley – his left leg and then his right leg moving towards the ceiling.

'*Heh*,' he said, 'these are words that I do not yet understand, but, Bwana, what I do understand is that my hips work. Behold, let me take my legs out of this plaster that I may bend my knees.'

'*Ng'o*, wait some days, and when we see the hips work, then we will work on the other portions, but still within your plaster make your muscles work. Pull your kneecap bone up, that's the way, do it over and over again.'

I was intrigued to see the way that N'yani held his mouth as he made his muscles work, controlling them one by one. Then he smiled:

'*Heh*, Bwana, this is a thing of wonder. It is altogether beyond the wisdom of our tribe.'

I moved across to the window and listened to the throb of drums. I turned back.

'Behold, I wish we had news of what is happening over there, or what has happened.'

'*Heh*, Bwana,' said N'yani, 'news will come.'

13

Witchdoctor's Futility

I was all impatient. First I tried to listen to some music on the gramophone but in the middle of the record I was irritated and turned it off. Then I sat down and tried to work out hospital statistics but it was hopeless. I turned up the lamp and tried to concentrate on reading the *Tanganyika Standard* but again I couldn't do it and got up and walked restlessly. Half-a-dozen times I looked at my watch. Time did not seem to move on. How I wished for action of some sort. If only they'd call me to the hospital to a difficult case.

Out in the thornbush a hyena howled dismally. In the bright moonlight I could just see its shadow a good hundred yards away. I crept out of the door, got as near as I could, picked up a round stone and threw it with everything I had. I heard the stone land in the thornbush and to my satisfaction the hyena's howl stopped suddenly. This made me feel better. I walked up and down in the clearing outside my jungle home and watched clouds scurry across the moon. It was almost midnight. Jackals eerily called to one another on the fringe of the swamp and the fact of their voices moving further and further away was the first indication that I had that somebody must be coming up the path towards my house. Then I saw a figure moving in a way that stamped him as Hezeroni, the postman. At a steady jog-trot he came up the path and sat down on the step of my house, panting.

'*Yah*, Bwana, news. *Kah! Heh!* How I have run to bring you this news!'

I pumped up a primus stove and put the kettle on it.

'We will moisten your news, O Hezeroni, with tea.'

The postman stood to his feet. 'Bwana. *Kah*, things have been happening in the village of M'bovu. *Yoh!* And did I have difficulty to find out all the words? *Heh!* If I did not have relations in that village, and if they did not look to me to supply two cows towards a dowry, *hongo*, we would not have heard these words. This is what happened. Everything took place under that great baobab tree near the house of N'goma, the witchdoctor. *Hakali mitindo*, early in the morning, the boy was taken to N'goma. *Heh*, did he not try with strength to remove that *dudu*? Bwana, first he took a thorn. It was as long as this.' He held up his first finger. '*Yah*, Bwana, he took the boy and put his head on his knee, and he dug in the child's ear. At first the boy just set his teeth and said nothing, and then, Bwana, suddenly he screamed. *Yah*, the hand of N'goma is not gentle!'

'Truly, and the point of a thorn is not kind to his eardrum. *Yoh*, Hezeroni, what pain that boy must have suffered, and did N'goma shift the *dudu*?'

'*Uh, uh*, Bwana, the *dudu* remained there. Behold, there were many words. The Chief and witchdoctor and elders of the tribe talked while M'bangho sat in the shade, Bwana, his hand over his ear, looking, Bwana, just dreadful. *Heh*, his eyes looked like those that do not sleep. His very skin looked dull. Then, Bwana, they brought a goat. They killed it and made from its skin a charm that he should wear round his ankles and round his neck. As he stood up for those to be put on, suddenly he screamed, shook his head, and put his hand over his ear.

'*Yah*,' he said, 'it walks! It walks! *Ehh!* The pain!''

''*Hongo*,' said N'goma, 'the ancestors will cause it to walk from your ear.'

'Bwana, the *dudu* stayed tightly in the place of its choice. All day long the small drum of N'goma has been beaten, calling upon the ancestors, but, Bwana, the *dudu* still stays in the place of its choice. *Kah*, and M'bangho, he sleeps not; he rests not, Bwana; he cannot eat.

'And so it was at sundown that N'goma made more medicine. He took three *mafigo*, stones, between which the fire is made and upon which rests the clay pot for cooking. He put some of the stomach contents of the goat between them, and called upon the ancestors to bring success to his medicine pot. Into the pot, Bwana, went some fat of the goat, water and some of the things of wonder from his black box in which he keeps his special medicines. There was some of the substance that shines amongst the high rocks.' I knew he referred to some mica. 'And, Bwana, there were some roots of trees that he had dug in the jungle, and he cooked it, stirring and chanting to himself.'

Hezeroni paused to sip his tea, and I looked out over the cold whiteness of the plains in the moonlight and watched the shadow of a cloud move silently towards the village of M'bovu, and I thought of that child lying there suffering, and here was I, helpless, not because I hadn't the medicines and the instruments, but because there was a barrier of witchcraft, superstition, hostility, heathendom, through which I might not force my way. I walked up and down irritably. Hezeroni looked at me.

'*Kah*, Bwana, when Simba, the lion, is in *mtego*, the trap, does he not walk up and down aimlessly and use strength for no value? *Kah*, Bwana, drink your tea and relax. There are other ways of the strength of the lion showing itself. For instance, a strong hand removing the door of the trap.'

'*Kah*,' I said, 'Come on, O thou postman, thou carrier of written words, thou fountain of spoken words.'

'*Heh*,' he smiled, 'Bwana, six teaspoons of sugar, please.'

I poured out his second cup.

'*Heh*,' said Hezeroni, 'I was telling you, Bwana, that he cooked his medicine, then when it was boiling, he took a spoonful of it. First, he put on to his wrist the white round discs of his witchdoctor's office; the leopard-skin was round his loins. Behold, the teeth of the leopard also were hanging from his neck and round his head was cowskin. He stood there, Bwana, with his eyes gleaming, his shoulders seemed to shake and to shiver, and everyone was silent. He turned to M'bangho, beckoning with his hand, '*Uze*. Come!' The child came to him. Then '*down*' he ordered, and as the boy bent he grasped his head and held it firmly between his knees. He reached out with his wooden spoon for the medicine. It came all bubbling from the pot.'

'*Yah*,' I said, 'this is sheer wickedness, Hezeroni, pouring boiling . . .'

'*Kah*, Bwana, listen to me. Shall my words flow smoothly if your words get tangled with them?'

'Go on,' I said, 'go on, tell me.'

'Bwana, he took the boiling medicine. For a moment he held it poised and as he did so, the boy, out of the corner of his eye, saw what was happening. At the back of his head, Bwana, was one knee of the witchdoctor. Before his face, Bwana, was the other knee of the witchdoctor, holding him tightly. Courage, or fear, or both, Bwana, welled up in him. He saw what was coming and did all he could. He bit and bit hard. *Heeh*, the contents of that spoon went everywhere, some on the boy's face, some on N'goma's leg. *Yah*, Bwana, and did he roar with anger! The boy sprang to his feet and ran, Bwana. How he ran! N'goma picked up his medicine and threw it at the boy, but *yah*, Bwana, his feet were those of a *zimba*, the buck. *Heh*, and then there was a *shauri*. N'goma had great anger. He demanded that a cow should be given him because of the boy's action. *Heh*, and the great ones agreed. M'bovu himself had great anger and, Bwana, the words that I hear are that he thrashed the boy with a hippo-hide whip. They tell me the child lies on his mat, his skin throbbing from a whipping, his face burnt with the witchdoctor's medicine, and Bwana, the *dudu* still walks in his ear.'

Hezeroni paused dramatically, drank deeply from his cup and set it down.

'*Yah*, Bwana, and there is nothing you can do.'

'*Hongo*,' I said, 'there is. Come with me now.'

'Bwana, I will not go to that village. *Heh*, it would be murder.'

'I'm not going to the village. I'm going another way; a way of wisdom and a way of strength.'

We walked up to the hospital. There was the vague gleam of a hurricane light in the men's ward. I went to Daudi's house.

'*Hodi*?' I cried.

A sleepy voice came from inside. '*Nhawule*, what's up?'

'It is I, Daudi.'

'*Heeh*,' said the voice, '*nili meso*, my eyes are open.'

A minute later he appeared.

'Come with me to where Simba lies. I would have prayer at this hour for young M'bangho.'

A few minutes later we were around Simba's bed, talking in whispers, telling the story of what had happened.

Then I saw N'yani open his eyes.

'*Kah*,' he yawned, 'Bwana, the child will die.'

'*Uh, uh*,' I said, 'We will pray and ask God. Does He not say, "When two or three of you are gathered together, there am I in the middle?"'

N'yani looked round fearfully.

'Bwana, is He here?'

I nodded.

'But there is no fear of Him when He is the Saviour Who takes away your sin. When He is your Guide Who shows you the way to walk in life, you have no fear of Him.'

'*Kah*,' said N'yani, 'but He is not that to me.'

'He is that to us,' said Simba. 'Listen, we will speak to Him.'

In simple words we prayed for that child and asked God somehow to let us help him. As we got up from our knees, Daudi said, 'I was reading tonight, Bwana, that when the followers of Jesus were with Him, Jesus said to them, in a problem just like this, "Do you believe that I am able to do this?" His followers said, "Yes, Lord," and Jesus said, "Right, according to your faith it shall be done."'

I walked out into the bright moonlight, watching the clouds scud past the full moon. Hezeroni walked silently with me for a while. Then he said, 'Bwana, do you not understand my words now about the lion and the trap? If the hand of God opens the door of the trap then, behold, you will be able to help this child.'

'*Heh*, Hezeroni, that is so, but we must have much faith.'

14
Legs that Talk

The drums had been silent at M'bovu's village for two days now; a silence which I felt was ominous seemed to hover over that place. I found it hard to concentrate as I looked at Simba's temperature chart and noted with satisfaction that for days it had stayed down. My finger quested along the calf of his leg and under his knee; the swelling had disappeared.

'*Yah*,' said the hunter, 'Bwana, when may I get up?'

'Tomorrow,' I replied, 'but your legs must be bandaged so that you cannot walk fast.'

'*Heh*,' he said, 'Bwana, if I may put my feet on the ground I will have joy.'

In the next bed, N'yani was pulling his ropes. His feet were moving up and down rhythmically.

'Bwana,' he said, 'I have strength in my legs. Behold, I can move them in a way that I have not done for years.'

I moved across to him, and took off the long, gutter-like plaster splint that was supporting his legs. Slowly

he drew them up and slowly he stretched them out again with a huge smile on his face.

'Bwana, they're almost right. See, I can move them. May I not tomorrow also try to walk?'

'*Heh*,' said Daudi, 'you could not walk.'

'*Kumbe*,' said N'yani, 'I could walk if my hands were able to strengthen me.'

'*Hongo*,' I said, 'that's an idea.'

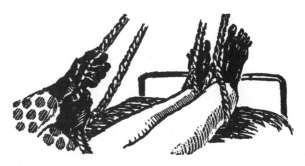

I thought of the two posts outside and as I looked at the great strength of his arms and shoulders, I thought that if a strong rope were firmly fixed between those two posts, he could hold on to it with his hands and take the main burden of his weight off his feet, and thus learn once again. I made a mental note to speak to Elisha about it. As I did so, my mind went back to the place beyond the baobab trees where young M'bangho was suffering intensely. I turned round to Simba.

'*Hongo*, it is good that you are better, and you too, N'yani, but I have discomfort in my mind when I think of that boy, the *dudu* in his ear, and the work of the witchdoctor. For some days now there has been no news.'

'Two days only, Bwana,' said Daudi.

'*Hongo*, and if you had a *dudu* in your ear for two days, would it seem but a short time?'

'*Kah*,' muttered Daudi, '*heh*, truly he suffers, that child.'

'And no word,' I said, 'not even a whisper of what is happening.'

Then came the small voice at the door, '*Hodi*?'

'*Yah*,' said N'yani, 'here comes my food and with it news.'

The small girl took the basket of porridge slowly from her head.

'*Yah*,' she said, 'behold, later today will be a thunderstorm. My head throbs. *Hongo*, and the whole village of M'bovu seems just like that. *Kah*, it is a strange thing. *Heh*, it all seems to be filled with sullen anger. Few words are spoken, Bwana, but the great ones of the village talk together and talk in whispers. *Heh*, Bwana, last night in the dusk as they cooked their food, I walked beside the house of M'bovu and I listened at the wall, at the place where M'bangho lies. *Kah*, and I could hear groanings – groanings, Bwana, without strength.'

'*Yah*,' said N'yani, 'kumbi yali wumi, he is alive at least.'

The small girl nodded.

'There is no further news,' she said, as quietly she made her departure.

'Hezeroni may have more news,' I said, but he came in the evening with a long face.

'Bwana, there is nothing to tell. Nobody knows anything except that M'bovu talks with the old men of the tribe and they have reached no agreement. Of what they are speaking, nobody knows.'

Another day of silence went by.

I kept looking at that village and wondering. The day was so full that I didn't have much chance to think, for Elisha had fixed up a rope outside the ward, and walking more by touch than anything, N'yani swung himself along. Every now and then he rested

his weight on his feet. At the beginning his knees gave under him, but later in the afternoon he showed me how he had learned to control his knees. Everybody was most intrigued with his form, including Simba, who walked along with both his knees firmly tied up in large bandages. Twice that day, in between incidents, Daudi and I knelt together and asked God to help in the matter of young M'bangho. I saw Simba and Perisi sitting on stools under the pomegranate tree with their heads bowed and I knew that they too were praying. Folk all over the C.M.S. hospital were praying for that small boy. N'yani had noticed this as well.

'God is slow to answer prayer, Bwana.'

'*Heeh*, slow to me, yes, but I always know that God has a plan and when His time comes, then He works. His own words are these, "Do not be anxious about things, but in every item of your living, by praying and by asking for things and with saying thank you; in this way tell your needs to God."' (*I made a free translation of the African version of the New Testament.*)

'*Heh*,' said Simba, who had come up, 'Bwana, do that, and the peace of God fills your heart. I am confident that God is going to take action in the matter of M'bangho soon.'

'*Heh*,' said N'yani, 'I wonder.'

'Heh,' said a small voice behind us, 'behold, things are happening in the village of M'bovu.'

We jumped.

'*Yah*,' said N'yani, 'I did not hear you say "*Hodi*?"'

'*Kumbe*,' said the small girl, setting down his porridge in front of him. 'Behold, I cried "*hodi*?" twice, but you were talking with great strength. You did not hear my voice. It is even so with the old men at the village. *Kah*, they talk with strength. They shake their heads. *Heeh*, M'bovu sits there with his head in his hands and the old men talk to him. They would persuade him. Bwana, *heh*, they have solemn counsel, the old men of the village. *Yah*. They shake their heads and M'bovu waves his finger at them. N'goma shakes his finger at them. *Kah*, Bwana, their words are beyond my ear. The village is seething, Bwana, as porridge when it comes to the boil. Soon it will boil over and, *yah*, what then?'

'*Heh*,' said Daudi, 'Bwana, come over here into the centre of the *ibululu* where no one may hear us. N'yani has done great things. Everybody has been watching him. Among those who watched have been the spies of M'bovu, listening and watching everything. *Kah*, Bwana, we must be very careful. Behold, there is great fear in M'bovu's heart. He has anger with his son but he has fear now that his son will die. The medicines of *muganga* have shown little strength. The Chief has anger because he had to pay a cow for medicine that did not work. Also, he paid another cow because of the burning of *muganga* with his own medicine.

'*Yah*, I would like to have been there and seen that stuff spilt on the old man. *Yah, yah,* how he deserved it! *Kah*, Bwana, but he had anger. He demanded a cow. The cow was paid, but now there is a long discussion because N'goma says the cow that was given was diseased. He has great anger. He says that the *wulipicizo*, the compensation, is wrong and that this will cause the ancestors to be angry.'

'*Heh*,' said M'bovu, 'behold, the boy will die through the weakness of your medicine,' and then the old men will say, "The boy dies. Is he not in the line of chiefs of our village? Have you other sons? Does not the line of our chiefs go back to the days when the baobabs were young? *Heh*, and would you let this child die when the *muganga*, the witchdoctor, has stronger medicines?"'

'*Heh*,' says the old man, 'I shall make stronger medicines but my price is two cows – cows of strength, not diseased ones.'

'Then, Bwana, came another voice, '*Heh*, there are other medicines than those of the *muganga*. We have heard that N'yani, the cripple, whose legs were bent, now walks on straight legs. This is the work of the Bwana at the hospital of C.M.S. Are there not other ways? Behold, shall we not take the child to the hospital and let the Bwana try his medicines? If he can heal the legs of a cripple, behold, can he not remove a *dudu* from a child's ear?''

'*Hongo*, Daudi, how did you get all this information?'

'Bwana, it is as you say, you put three and three together.'

I smiled. '*Kah*, Daudi, but how do you make all this out?'

'Bwana, the wagging of the heads of the old men; the one old man who stands up and speaks. Is he not the one who had great trouble with his inside and was cured quickly with our needle? *Yah*, Bwana, we have built up strong friendships, which are deep and real but covered up, in many places of this country. Make no mistake.'

Suddenly Daudi drew me aside and took me to the dispensary. From the window you could see what was going on in the men's ward. Two old men, leaning on sticks, came up to the place.

'*Mbukwenyi*,' they said, 'Good-day.'

'*Mbukwa*,' replied Kefa.

'We would see N'yani.'

'*Hongo*,' said Kefa, 'you should watch him walk.'

From within the ward came a figure clinging to the door-post, to the window, and then reaching out a strong hand for the rope that went from post to post. Gripping this, and with his muscles showing out against his black skin, he walked, taking more and more weight on his legs as he moved.

'*Yah*,' he said with laughter in his voice, '*heh*, behold, N'yani, the monkey, walks; not only with his front feet, but with his back feet. *Yah*, this is the work of a strong medicine. *Heh*, behold, this outshines all the ways of the *waganga*.'

The old men nodded their heads slowly. '*Heeh*, this is a word of wisdom. *Kah*, do it for us again.'

N'yani did so, with a broad smile.

'*Heh*, truly, this is a word of wisdom,' they said. '*Kah*, do it for us again.'

N'yani did so, laughing as he took his hands away from the rope and stood swaying for a second.

'*Yah*,' he said, 'I stand. On my own feet.'

The old men talked together for a moment, nodded, and then said, '*Chokwiwona*, we will be seeing one another,' and moved away from the hospital.

'*Heh*,' said Daudi, 'those are some of the great ones of the tribe, the ones who live in the village of M'bovu, his chief advisers. They return to pour words into his ear.'

15
Answer

It was the late afternoon of the next day.

'*Heh*,' said Daudi, 'Bwana, no news yet of M'bangho.'

'*Kumbe*, perhaps you were wrong in what you thought, Daudi.'

'Bwana, I think these words were right.'

We talked as we went over the instruments in the operating theatre – oiling the joints, polishing.

'*Kah*,' said Daudi, 'these are the things we would use, Bwana, if the opportunity came.' He picked up the crocodile forceps, putting a drop of oil in each of the joints and wiggling them to and fro. '*Yah*,' he said, 'remember the snake, Bwana? See, do not the forceps open and shut their mouth just like that snake of yours?'

'*Hongo*,' I said, 'I moved fast out of this room when I saw that snake down there, Daudi. *Heeh*, truly M'bovu is a man of wickedness, but he will yet have thankfulness that his snake did not strike.'

'*Kah*, Bwana, I feel sure that into your hands will come the opportunity of saving that boy's life.'

Daudi put the forceps back on the shelf and set to work to dismantle and clean the primus stove, while I sharpened a series of needles for injections. He turned to the window and looked out towards the baobab tree.

'*Hongo*, Bwana, look, look! There is a long safari of people. Who they are I cannot tell from here, but *yah*, Bwana, it may be . . . '

'Run to my office and get the telescope which is in the second drawer on the left-hand side.'

Daudi was out of the door like a shot and I could hear his feet padding up the dry path. Perhaps two miles away from us, coming along like a drawn-out mobile queue, were some twenty people, moving from the direction of M'bovu's village. There was an odd bulge at the end of this group of people which might mean anything. Daudi was at my side with the telescope. I focused it and looked for a long minute.

'*Kah*, Bwana, may I see too?'

I handed over the instrument and the dispenser looked with interest.

'*Kah*, Bwana, truly, that is M'bovu in front. See the red fez on his head and his khaki *kanzu*. *Heh*, behind him come the old men that were here yesterday who saw N'yani. I know their walk, Bwana, one limps.'

'What's that right at the back, at the end of them? Do you think, Daudi . . .?'

'*Heh*, Bwana, it is as though they led someone or carried them. *Heh*, it is a man with his arm round the shoulders of a boy. It is M'bangho, Bwana. They do not carry him; he walks.'

Others had noticed what was happening. Sechelela and Perisi came in through the door.

'Bwana,' they said, 'they're coming. Truly, God has heard our words.'

Then Simba's deep voice came at the door.

'*Hodi*, Bwana, *hodi*?'

'*Karibu*,' I replied. 'Come in.'

'Bwana, they're coming. I have seen them. *Heh*; in front comes M'bovu himself. Truly, God has heard our prayers. *Yah*, now all you have to do is to remove the insect.'

'*Heeh*, all I have to do is to remove the insect! Come on, my friends, while we are here, let us pray and talk to God and ask for His help.'

So round that operating table, again we prayed for guidance for my hand in the work that lay ahead.

'*Heh*,' said Simba, 'you might watch carefully the words of M'bovu. He is full of subtlety, even as *nzoka*, the snake.'

'*Kah*,' said Daudi, 'and you, Simba, and you, Perisi, had better not be where people can see you.'

'*Ngheeh!*' nodded Sechelela. 'True, but let them see N'yani. *Kah*, he is the one of whom they will speak. Make no mistake about that, Bwana.'

We all went our several ways and I sat in my office pretending to fill in Government forms. This I did quite unsuccessfully, and then came a voice at the door.

'*Hodi*, Bwana, *hodi*? May we come in?'

'*Karibu*,' I replied, and in came M'bovu and two of the elders of his tribe. With them came Daudi.

'Bwana,' said M'bovu, 'I have come to greet.'

'*Hongo*,' I said, raising my eyebrows politely.

'*Heh,*' said the two old men, 'also we would have joy to see N'yani, whose legs have gained strength again.'

M'bovu nodded his head. 'Bwana, we would see this thing. It is one of wonder, because all of our village thought that his legs had lost their strength. Truly, your medicine is to be praised.'

'*Kumbe,*' said Daudi, 'the Bwana would have joy to take you to see N'yani.'

So we all adjourned to the veranda of the men's ward where N'yani, highly delighted, was giving a demonstration of his ability to walk. About a hundred people must have gathered by this time. Notwithstanding Daudi's best efforts, there was a feeling of tension in the air. I whispered into his ear.

'What about the boy? Shouldn't we get on to this at once?'

'*Uh, uh,*' said Daudi, shaking his head. 'Behold, Bwana, we have a proverb, "Hurry, hurry has no blessing".'

'That's all right for you, but if you had a *dudu* in your ear ...?'

'*Huh*, Bwana, five minutes is small time when you think the *dudu* has been there five days. Spend a little more time in words.'

I went across to M'bovu.

'*Mbukwa*, Chief, would you care to see where we make our medicines?'

'*Heh,*' he said, without much enthusiasm, '*heh*, I will come.'

I took him to the door of the dispensary and showed him the bottles, the great tins filled with ointment and cough mixture, the preparation for injection.

'*Hongo,*' he said, 'there is much medicine here.'

Some of the old men peered over his shoulder. One said:

'*Heh*, it was the medicine in the small bottle that they gave me. *Yoh*, and it had strength.'

The Chief gave him a sharp look and the old man suddenly fell silent.

'This is the room,' I said, 'where we find the *dudus*, the germs that cause trouble in many diseases.' I pointed out the microscope, the various bottles and the various stains.

'*Heh*,' he said, 'it is a place of witchcraft.'

'*Kah, ng'o*, this is a place of wisdom,' said Daudi.

M'bovu shrugged his shoulders and I felt that things were coming to a head. Suddenly there was a disturbance on the veranda.

'*Yah*,' said a voice, '*heh*, he has fallen.'

Young M'bangho had fainted and if it hadn't been for the strong arm of Simba he would have fallen flat on the concrete.

Simba looked with smouldering eyes at the Chief.

'*Hongo*,' I said, 'the child is ill?'

'*Heh, heh*,' said the Chief, '*yali yatamigwe*, he has sickness.'

M'bovu turned round with a slight sneer on his face.

'*Magu gwe gwe*, that is your affair. Is it my work to tell of sicknesses to one who can make the lame walk?'

I whispered to Daudi. He went at a run to the dispensary, coming back with a syringe. The needle was thrust home. In a matter of seconds the boy sat up. I put my arm behind him to steady him.

'*Yoh*,' I turned to M'bovu with a hard note in my voice, 'great one, tell me the truth. What is this boy's trouble?'

The Chief moved from one foot to the other.

'*Eh*,' he said, 'he was well this morning. Behold, he came here and then he ...'

Daudi saw the smouldering hostility in Simba's eyes. He saw also that I was going to say something which he feared might start trouble.

Hastily he said, 'Bwana, the child has sickness. Let us take him into the room where we deal with those who are as he is.'

I picked the boy up and carried him in. With us came Samson and Kefa. The door was closed.

'*Yah*,' hissed Daudi. 'Heh, Bwana, truly he is a man of evil.'

I turned to the boy. 'Tell me your trouble.'

'Bwana,' he said, 'I am near to death. *Heh*, I have tiredness. *Yah*, Bwana, it is this number of days (he held up five fingers) since a *dudu* got into my ear. It walks in my ear. Even now it walks. *Yah*, the pain, Bwana. My head throbs and throbs and throbs. There is a noise in my ear as though a great drum were beaten. *Kah*, Bwana, I am going to die. Help me! Oh, help me!'

'I'll do that,' I replied, and picked up my auriscope, the special variety of instrument which enabled me to look right into a person's ear; a tiny torch bulb, battery-lighted, giving me just sufficient light to see. The ear was swollen, nothing was visible. I put in some local anaesthetic and another medicine to reduce the swelling quickly.

As Daudi poured out a strong dose of medicine to strengthen the lad, I said, 'In a few moments now we will be able to help you. Let the medicines work, but, tell me, how did the *dudu* get in?'

'Bwana, I lay on my cowskin on the floor. Behold, as I slept the dudu came into my ear. *Hongo*, it was easy for it to get in.'

'Was it easy to get it out?'

'*Yah*,' said the boy, with a trace of a smile at the corner of his mouth, 'Bwana, it has been a tremendous work to try and get it out.'

'It was easy to get in, hard to get rid of, *eh*? Does it make you miserable?'

'*Kah*, Bwana, does it make me miserable!!' He rolled his eyes.

'*Kah*,' said Daudi, '*that's* it, Bwana, that's it … easy to get into you, can't get rid of it by yourself, makes you miserable all the time it's there … that's sin all right.'

The boy looked at us not understanding.

'*Kah*,' said Daudi, 'these are the words, Bwana. When we go outside, let me speak to them. Let me tell them that sin pays its servants.'

'*Heh, kumbe*, the wage is death,' agreed Simba.

'Let me tell them, Bwana, that God frees from sin, and gives to those who serve Him, and His gift for which you pay nothing is eternal life. All this because of what Jesus Christ did for us. Bwana, these are the words I read today.'

I had another look at the boy's ear. It was almost possible to get to work and remove the *dudu*.

'Right,' I said, 'come on. We will start.'

16
Out

'Forceps, please, Daudi. Kefa, I want a small bowl of swabs and that bottle of yellow medicine to put drops into his ears when I have finished.'

I turned to scrub my hands before removing the *dudu*.

'Bwana,' said he, '*heh*, never have days and nights gone so slowly as these last five. *Yah*, should you fail in the work that you are doing and the *dudu* remain in my ear, kumbe, I will die.'

I picked up the auriscope, switched on the minute light which it contained and looked into his ear. He clenched his teeth. Looking down the swollen passage to his eardrum I could just see the broad black back of an insect completely blocking the ear.

Daudi's voice came urgently behind me.

'Bwana, do not do this work in here.'

'But it's better in here. I've got everything convenient. There are the swabs, the instruments. The sterilizer is here. The table is a convenient one. The light is good.'

'Bwana, but in here there are few of us, all of us who understand the hospital, but out there there are many people who do not understand. Do it outside; let everyone see, Bwana. Let them see that they may understand the way of wisdom of the hospital. Think how much good can be done by the scores of tongues which will wag after today's work. *Heh*, surely this work will be talked about over and around every campfire in Ugogo for many days, Bwana.'

Kefa joined in.

'*Heh*, these are words of truth. N'goma's work is hidden, Bwana. It is mystic. It is in the dark. But yours, *kumbe!* It is in the light. We have nothing to hide. We have nothing to lose, Bwana, and we have everything to gain. Also there will be the opportunity of telling them the words that really matter.'

I picked up the auriscope in one hand and the crocodile forceps in the other.

'All right. Let's go out there.'

So we went out on the veranda. The people crowded round. Kefa placed a three-legged stool for M'bangho and another one for me.

Daudi held a tray which was cut from a kerosene tin and in it were the various things that I would require for this minor operation. Through the window behind me, I could see N'yani and Simba looking across at a group of seated Africans. In front, on stools, sat M'bovu and the elders of the tribe. Behind them were a number of Africans with red mud in their hair, clutching hunting spears or knobbed sticks. These were the folk from M'bovu's village, and there were crowds of people. Small boys and girls wormed their way to the front. Some women with baskets on their heads stopped to watch. Everybody was intensely interested.

'*Kumbe*,' I said, 'before I do this work, shall we not ask the help of God?'

In a very simple, direct way Daudi prayed that God would help us to help M'bangho and others, by what was about to be done.

There was a restlessness amongst M'bovu's people as we prayed, but everything became quiet and still as I switched on again the light of the auriscope and peered into the boy's ear. This was no easy business because his fatigue made it almost impossible for him to keep his head still, and as I peered, his head moved away from me.

'*Yah*, M'bangho, it is no easy matter to hunt *dudus* in people's ears, and *yah*, if you have to chase the head as well, *heh*, it is a double trouble.'

'*Kumbe*, Bwana,' said the boy, 'I want to help, but *eh*, I'm tired, so tired.'

'*Heh*,' said Daudi, 'rest your head against the wall and then it cannot move, also set your teeth and the Bwana will work with speed.'

The boy did so. Again I looked through the auriscope into the ear. I could see the place where the witchdoctor's thorn had stabbed. The side of the boy's face was burnt by the witchdoctor's medicine, and there, deeply in the ear, was the *dudu* that had caused all the trouble, clinging tightly to the eardrum, obviously reluctant to leave its place. It had swollen considerably since the day it got in.

'*Yah*,' said a voice behind me, 'see, it is an instrument of wonder that the Bwana has. See how it opens and shuts.'

I moved it up and down a few times for them to see what I was going to do, and then I put it through the aurisope and tried to grab the insect. The smoothness of its back made this difficult. A groan came from M'bangho.

'*Yah*, Bwana, there is pain. There is pain.'

'*Kah*,' said M'bovu, 'the child has no pain.'

'*Heh*,' through the window came a voice (which I suspected as being Simba's), '*hongo*, the Chief has no *dudu* in his ear.'

There was a titter in the background. I put my hand on M'bangho's shoulder.

'Have a rest for a moment,' I said, 'then, next time, I want you to cough, because when you cough your eardrum moves ever so slightly. This may upset the *dudu's* hold.'

A few seconds later the boy swallowed and said, '*Tayari*, Bwana.'

He set his teeth and put his head firmly against the wall and coughed.

Looking down the auriscope I could see the insect suddenly seem to turn a little on its side and its feet came into view. I prodded at the creature with forceps. It turned a little bit more. Suddenly my opportunity came and I closed the jaws of the crocodile forceps on the *dudu's* leg. Never have I had more satisfaction in pulling a leg!

I had to work with extreme care. I could hear the whispers from the crowd behind me.

'*Hongo!* It is a work of difficulty.'

The tick moved sideways a little, giving me just the opportunity I wanted and I quickly shifted my grip to the creature's body and with a considerable amount of satisfaction withdrew from M'bangho's ear the tick, its legs wriggling violently in the grip of the crocodile forceps.

'*Yoh*,' breathed all the group, '*heeh*, the Bwana has succeeded. Look at it. Behold how it wriggles!'

M'bangho was caressing his ear.

'*Yah*,' he said, '*heeh. Kah.*' And then, 'Bwana, look again with your little lamp. Perhaps the *dudu* has other relations.'

I looked, and apart from the swollen eardrum, there was nothing left. I put in some of the yellow drops. An enthusiastic murmur of voices came from those watching, but M'bangho had eyes for the dudu and the dudu only.

'Bwana,' he said between clenched teeth, 'give it to me.'

Smiling I did so and put it on his thumb. He placed it on his nail and looked at it.

'*Yah*,' he fixed his gaze on it, 'for five days you made my life a misery. *Heh.*' Then with a slow smile he brought his other thumbnail into play and crushed the *dudu*. There was a roar of laughter.

'*Heh*,' they said, 'the *dudu* is no more.'

Daudi was on his feet. '*Kumbe*,' he said, 'was it easy for the *dudu* to get into the ear?'

'*Heeh*,' they said, all nodding vigorously.

M'bangho nodded his head also, feelingly.

'Could the boy get rid of it himself?'

'*Uh, uh*,' came the reply, with a concerted shaking of heads.

'Could you remove it, O Great One?' Daudi turned to M'bovu, who shook his head.

There was a broad grin on Simba's face and I heard a whisper, 'Not even by blowing in the other ear, or standing him on his head and shaking him! *Kah*, what a way of wisdom.'

Daudi's voice went on. 'Could N'goma, the witchdoctor, get rid of the *dudu* from the boy's ear?'

A sudden bleak silence fell on the small group there but M'bangho's voice came strongly.

'*Uh, uh*, he could not.'

'*Hoh*,' said Daudi, 'who could then?'

'*Kumbe*,' said the boy, 'the Bwana with his *cuma* – his iron thing of great wisdom. He got rid of it.'

'*Ooooh!*' Daudi raised his eyebrows. 'Tell me, M'bangho, did you have joy while the *dudu* was in your ear?'

'*Heh*,' said the boy, 'did I not have great pain? Did I not have the fears of death?'

'*Kumbe*,' Daudi waved his finger, 'listen to my riddle. What is it that is easy to get into you, you can't get rid of by yourself, that your relations can't get rid of, your ancestors can't get rid of, the witchdoctor can't get rid of, a thing that always makes you miserable, a thing that always kills you in the long run – what is its name?'

'*Kumbe,*' said N'yani from the window, 'surely is it not a *dudu* that gets in a boy's ear?'

'*Heh,*' said Daudi, 'it is more than that. It is the *dudu* of sin that gets into everybody's life. It gets in with ease. It is in the heart of every man and we ourselves cannot get rid of it. Try as we will, we cannot buy it out of us. We cannot get it out with charms. The Bwana here cannot get rid of it for us, but only Jesus, the Son of God, Who lived that we might understand God, Who died that our sins might be taken away. He only can take that *dudu* of sin from our hearts.'

I saw some of those Africans with red mud in their hair nodding their heads. They had understood this practical parable. M'bovu got to his feet and started to talk.

'*Kumbe,*' he said, 'the ways of the Bwana are greatly to be praised. His medicine is very strong. It has brought great help to our tribe. We have much praise for him.'

'Great One,' I said, 'if you have praise, then show your appreciation by letting the people of your tribe come to our hospital.'

Elisha, the carpenter, suddenly turned to M'bovu.

'Great One, will you not show your thanks to the Bwana by a gift?'

M'bovu looked uncomfortable. He feared another cow would shortly leave his herd. I turned to him.

'Great One, may I ask that your thanks be shown by allowing M'bangho to come and play football with those of the hospital?'

'*Heh,*' said the Chief, 'Bwana, it shall be as you ask.'

I could hear Simba's quickly indrawn breath behind me. The Chief got to his feet.

'*Lyaswa*, the sun has set,' he said. 'We must return.'

'Truly,' I said, 'but M'bangho shall remain here for two days that we may make sure that the *dudu* produces no further trouble.'

For a minute the Chief hesitated, but as he looked at those who were with him he saw their meaning glances and nodded saying, '*Kwaheri*, goodbye.'

As they moved on in the gloaming Daudi said, 'Do not forget this riddle – "it is easy to get in, but you can't get rid of it by yourself, that *dudu* called sin".'

17

Two Ways

'Give M'bangho a tablespoon full of the green mixture, Daudi.'

'*Heh*, Bwana, the medicine that brings sleep to the eyes?'

I nodded. 'It also brings comfort to the ears, Daudi.'

'*Heh*,' yawned M'bangho, 'all I need, Bwana, is a place on which to put my head, another place on which to put my back, and I will sleep. *Heh*, it is joy to lie without a *dudu* in your ear. *Yah*, Bwana, *heh*, I have great thanks. *Uh, ahhhh*,' he yawned again.

'*Kumbe*, Bwana, they were true words when you said that there is joy when it is gone.' He gulped down the green medicine with a wry face. '*Ugh, heh*, it is salty, Bwana.' He yawned again.

'Get into bed. We will cover you with blankets. You will sleep.'

'*Kah*,' said the boy, 'Bwana, *dudus* in the ear bring no joy. *Dudus* out of the ear … *kah*, how happy I am.'

'*Hongo*,' said Daudi, 'and don't forget, just the same …'

But M'bangho was already asleep. He just flopped on to the bed and was immediately unconscious.

'*Heh*,' said Simba looking down at him, 'that child had fatigue, fatigue so great, Bwana, that you couldn't measure it. *Heh*, so tired is he that he would not wake if he heard the sound of porridge being cooked.'

'*Heh*,' said Daudi, 'you, if you heard the sound of porridge being scraped, would wake in the middle of the night.'

'*Yah*,' said Simba, '*yah*, when it comes to feasts, Bwana, *heh*, truly I know my way about.'

'*Heeh*,' said Daudi, but Simba was tapping me on the shoulder.

'Bwana, he could go two ways, this boy. His father's way or the way that we follow here at the hospital, and I want to make him understand in a way that he will not forget. Behold, the *dudu* has made him understand many things, but I would also have him understand clearly that there are two ways he can go. Tomorrow I would tell you all the story.'

'*Kah*,' said Daudi, 'is it about food?'

'*Heeh*,' said Simba, 'it is about food.'

Early next morning I went to the ward. M'bangho was lying in almost the same position as I had left him the day before, sound asleep. It was nearly midday when a lad rubbing his eyes came round to where I was working.

'Bwana,' he said, 'I have slept, *heh*. *Kah*, how I slept.' He yawned again. 'Bwana, my ear has not pain. Will you look into it with your small lantern?'

I took my auriscope, turned on the battery and looked into his ear. It was swollen and red but definitely improving. I put in more drops. He held his head on one side, swaying his ear around.

'*Yah*, Bwana, behold, this is medicine of comfort. The pain disappears.'

Through the window I saw Simba and Daudi come along and squat in the shade of the veranda.

'*Mbukwa*,' said Simba to the boy beside him.

'*Mbukwa*,' the boy replied.

'*Zo wugono*, how did you sleep?' asked Simba.

'*Hah*,' replied M'bangho, 'sleep? Oh, it was beautiful. Even now' – he yawned – '*ooh*, the pain is dying. *Kah*, that is medicine.'

A slow smile came over his face.

'The first time for days, behold, my stomach calls for food.'

'*Yah*,' said Simba, 'have I not a story to tell of *sungara*, the rabbit, and *ihowe*, the crow? Were they not invited, both of them, to a wedding feast?'

About a dozen folk had come around and were listening. Old Sechelela leant up against one of the posts of the veranda, and said:

'Bwana, in our country the rabbit is said to have wisdom, whereas *ihowe*, the crow, is one of small wisdom. *Kah*, it always seems to me the other way round.'

Simba was going on. '*Hongo*, and the very next day, after his first wedding invitation, another invitation came. Two wedding feasts on the same day. *Kah*, what a matter for thought! *Heh*, what a problem calling for the scratching of the head. *Kumbe*, *ihowe*, the crow, his mouth watering in happy anticipation, said to himself, "*Heh*, what's to stop me going to one, and then to the other? I shall be able to have two lovely feasts, *yah!*" and he laughed within himself.

'Many days he thought of these words and laughed within his heart. The day of the *sikuku* arrived, and both *sungura* and *ihowe* set out on their safari. They came to the place where the way forked. "*Ukubita hayi*, where are you going?" asked *ihowe*. The rabbit replied, "*Ku mwezi,* to the west, crow." Seeing his companion hesitate he said, "*Kwaheri*, goodbye," and went on with his safari. *Ihowe* unfortunately was now of two minds as to which feast he should go to first. The drums started to beat for the one feast, to the east by the baobab tree. He said within himself, "I will go there," and had just started to go along that road, when, *kumbe*, the drums on the western side, amongst the thornbush, began their beating. Throb, throb, throb! *Yah*, there he stood, the place where the road forked, wanting first to go to the east, *heh*, and then the west. His right foot was on one path and his left foot on the other. His eyes rolled in circles. The right foot came along the path to the east. *Yah*, and the left foot moved along the path to the west, but still he could not make up his mind to which feast to go first. The drums beat, and beat and beat, and they beat on both sides of him. They got louder and louder and louder. The black, beady eyes of the crow rolled mightily in his head. He opened and shut his mouth many times. *Kumbe*, but he was unable to decide, and all the time he tried to move down both paths at once, his feet getting ever wider apart, wider with each step that he took. *Heh*, and at last the drums beat very loudly indeed. What could he do? Was it not

a dilemma? He knew that if he didn't go to one of them before the drums stopped, *kumbe*, he wouldn't be able to get to a feast at all. His feet were now too far apart for him to think of flying, and while he was still wondering what he should do, the drums stopped.'

There was silence for a second and then M'bangho asked: '*Heeh*, and is that why, when a crow is on the ground his feet are always so far apart, *heh*?'

'*Hahh*,' nodded Simba, 'that is the reason. *Kumbe*, see there.'

Walking towards us along the dusty path, outside the dispensary, was a large black crow, his beady eyes rolling, his legs far apart.

'*Heh*,' said M'bangho, 'behold, *ihowe* is a creature of small wisdom. He eats dirt and filth. His voice is not music in the ear.'

'*Heh*,' said Simba, 'truly he is a bird of small wisdom who lives a life of small comfort. Is it not a true saying that you can't go to two places at the same time? *Hongo*.'

'And *hongo*,' said Daudi, 'those are words of truth. You cannot go to two places at the same time.'

M'bangho had a puzzled look on his face.

I turned to Daudi.

'Get me two stools – the three-legged ones that the *fundi*, the expert, makes down in the village.'

Two stools were brought.

'Behold, I would tell you this story in another way. There are two stools. We put them side by side. Simba, you are a man of strength. Sit on both those stools at once.'

'*Kah*,' said Simba, 'that is a thing of ease.'

Gently he lowered his twelve stone of bone and muscle on to the middle between those two stools, and then with a comical look on his face, let out a yell as the stools slipped on each side and he landed hard on the floor.

'*Yah*,' he said, '*kah, heeh!*'

M'bangho laughed, and clapped his hands. '*Yah*,' he said, '*heh*, you cannot sit on two stools at once.'

'Simba,' I said, 'sit on one stool and see if it is safe.'

Gingerly the hunter did so.

'Now sit on the other.'

He did so. He stood up suddenly. 'M'bangho, do you see it? *Ihowe*, the crow had to choose which way to go – I could not sit on two stools at once. Each one of us must decide which stool he will sit on, which path he will tread. When you had the dudu in your ear, you chose the path that would get rid of your pain. Behold, there is a bigger path looming up in front of you. I travelled this road and I saw that I could travel that way - it was God's way, it would take us to heaven. Jesus, the Son of God, beckoned me along that path, but beckoning down the other path was *Shaitani*, the devil. He winked with his eyes and called out alluring things. For a time I hesitated and then I travelled the road that went uphill with the Son of God. *Yah*, and it is the way of joy. You, too, must choose.'

At that moment an African with red mud in his hair and a spear in his hand walked up.

'*Mbukwa*,' he said.

'*Mbukwa*,' we replied.

'I have come from the Chief, M'bovu. He seeks news of his son.'

'The news is good,' I replied.

'The Chief desires that his son should return to his *kaya*, his home.'

'*Hongo*,' I said, 'it would be better to stay another night, to have more medicine in the ear.'

'These are the words of the Chief,' said the messenger.

'Bwana,' whispered M'bangho, 'it would be better if we followed his words. Behold, perhaps then he will let me come to play football.'

'*Heeh*,' nodded Simba, 'perhaps he will let M'bangho go to school. That will give him more chance to choose which way he will go.'

18
Clock Races

N'yani, the cripple, had recovered. His legs were somewhat thin but he could walk. It had taken eight months for this to happen, eight months during which the crocodile forceps sat unused in their cupboard in the operating theatre.

Another eight months went by – hectic months with work piling up in our jungle hospital. Lives were saved every week in that operating theatre. Practically every instrument we had was used over and over again, but the crocodile forceps sat quietly in a corner, only disturbed when they were oiled every Thursday. The rains came and an epidemic of meningitis. The hospital was on the move day and night. Time, clouded with fatigue, seemed to flow by month after month.

One late afternoon Daudi took up the operation book and wrote 'tropical ulcers, very strong.' I thought how right he was. 'Three treated with sulphanilamide.' He turned from the book and looked through the window.

'Bwana, you remember the day when we saw that procession of people coming up the hill from M'bovu's village?' He went over to the cupboard and picked up the crocodile forceps.

'*Yah*, Bwana, every time I have oiled these, I have prayed for M'bangho. I have prayed that God would help him to understand about the *dudu* of sin but, *yah*, I have heard not a word of him. It is said his father has sent him away many days' safari. *Kah!* The work of the hospital has been very strong, Bwana. We have had little time to rest for many days. *Yah*, it has been work, work, work. *Heeh*.' He yawned. 'Bwana, I would like time to rest, to rest away from all this, where people cannot come and say, "Daudi, get the operating theatre ready. We have an urgent case." Where people cannot come and say, "Daudi, prepare needles for injections." Where people cannot come and say, "Daudi, will you make special medicine? *Yah*, this is a place of much work."'

I smiled. 'What about a day off? I want to go on Saturday to Dodoma. There is a football match between the boys of the C.M.S. School and the soldiers of the King's African Rifles.'

'*Yah*, to see a football match would be good, Bwana. Behold, Simba would come also.'

I nodded.

So it was that we got into the old car and drove the thirty miles over the plains of Central Africa to the railway line which linked the Indian Ocean with Lake Tanganyika. About three miles from the hospital we came face to face with a lioness and two cubs. A mile further on three giraffes peered down at us from their vantage point above the thornbush and at least a dozen baboons scurried away as we crossed the dry river-bed.

'*Yah*,' said Simba, 'Bwana, today the whole jungle is at play.'

The car swung downhill, the dust of the road coming up in clouds. An African riding a donkey swerved away to one side of the road waving his hand. I recognized a patient of mine – Yacobo, by name. Women carrying gourds full of water on their heads clasped them and scurried from the middle of the road on to the side. Knob-billed birds screeched discordantly and flapped away into the thornbush, while overhead, one particular group of tall thorntrees were literally alive with weaver birds. The little fellows seemed to have used every available twig to build their admirable nests.

The grim outline of the fort which had been built in the days when Tanganyika was German East Africa loomed up ahead of us, and then swinging hard to the left through a cactus-lined path we came to the football ground. Africans, bare-footed, were kicking the soccer ball around in a highly expert way. The whistle blew for the beginning of the game and the King's African Rifles stalwarts, many of them over six feet, seemed to tower over the schoolboys who, however, were very nippy and nimble, particularly one lad – the centre half – who played splendidly.

Daudi and Simba were very excited about something. They seemed to have special interest in this boy. The crowd of Africans, Indians, Arabs, Somalilanders and a handful of Government officials vigorously cheered.

Halfway through the game I turned to Daudi.

'That lad playing centre half; now he's the sort of lad we should have at the hospital. See, he gets knocked

down – he's up. He's on the ball, he's nippy, he's keen, he's worth watching.'

'*Heh, heh*,' said Simba, rolling his eyes. 'He's one we ought to have at the hospital, truly.'

Daudi grinned and nodded knowingly.

'Bring him along at the end of the match. I'd like to have words with him.'

And so it was, at the end of the game, that an African lad, puffing a little from exertion, stood before me, standing rigidly at attention.

'Good afternoon, sir,' he said, and then in Chigogo, '*Mbukwa*, Bwana, do you remember me?'

I looked at him. His face was familiar but somehow my memory did not bring it clearly into focus.

'Yes,' I said, 'I remember you, but just where I saw you last, I can't remember.'

His face burst into a smile. He put his thumbnails together as though crushing something between them.

'*Yah*,' I said. '*Kah*, I remember you. Why, you're M'bangho! Did we not remove the *dudu* from your ear? Where have you been these many days?'

'My father sent me to my relations.' He pointed with his chin. 'Right over there. I went for many days but I managed to go to school and this month I have come here to the C.M.S. High School. Hah, Bwana, I have joy to see you. That was a work that you did – you and your crocodile forceps. *Kah*, that was the biggest day of my life, when you removed that *dudu* from my ear. *Heeh*, I had no joy, Bwana. The dudu was killing me. *Kah*, that was a sermon.'

I looked from Daudi to Simba. 'A sermon,' I said, 'no, it was a surgical operation.'

'*Ah*,' said the boy, 'you preached very strongly with your forceps that day, Bwana. You asked me was it easy for the *dudu* to get into the ear. *Kah*, and how easy it was!

'You told me that I could not get rid of the *dudu* by myself.

'*Yah*, and how well I knew that!

'You told me that the *dudu* was making me miserable, and that in the end it would have killed me.

'These were words that I knew. Then Simba here said that the *dudu* and its works were like sin.

'Daudi said the same and carried the story on. He said how sin got into you very easily but you couldn't get rid of it yourself, and he told how the strong Son of God died a criminal's death to get rid of sin from our hearts. He said how witchdoctors couldn't get rid of it, nor could the Chief. And, Bwana, I thought of these words very strongly.'

He paused for breath and turned around to Simba with a smile.

'And I also thought of the words of a story you told about *ihowe*, the crow, and his many relations, who always stand with their legs wide apart. I think of how *ihowe* had his chance but he could not make up his mind. Behold, he missed his opportunity.

'*Heh*, would I try and go God's way and the devil's way at once? And I said, "*Uh, uh*, behold I will follow God's way." My father allowed me to come here. Bwana, I am preparing, for one day I plan to come to the hospital, to work like Daudi works, that I too may help other people like you helped me.'

The whistle was blown and he said, 'Excuse me, Bwana. I must go to be with my people,' and ran off.

'*Kah*,' said Daudi, 'Bwana, that was a sermon. Behold, no doubt the crocodile forceps preached a much better sermon than did our tongues.'

'*Heh*,' said Simba, 'did we not pray and ask God to make things stick in his mind?'

Time passed. Five new calendars had hung on the dispensary wall between that day and another day when I looked through the window of the pathology room. An African was looking down the eyepiece of the microscope.

'*Heh*, Bwana,' he said, 'I find the work of the tick in this man's blood. See.'

I focused up and down and could see the minute purple corkscrew-like affairs that produce the disease known as tick fever.

'*Hongo*,' I said. 'Do you remember the day …?'

'*Heh*, Bwana, the day when I had i*kutupa*, the tick, in my ear, and you got rid of it with the crocodile forceps?' He ground his thumb-nails together reminiscently. 'Bwana, will I ever forget the day! *Yah*, it was the time when I chose which way I would go. The road forked that day and I chose the way that led to God.'

He got up from his seat, cleaned the lens of the microscope, put it away in the box, wrote in the book and closed it.

'Bwana,' he said, 'that is the last time I will do this work. Behold, tomorrow I go to my village to be Chief in place of my father. *Yah*, he would not follow the ways of wisdom, and he has been gathered to his ancestors, and now I am to be Chief in his place.'

I looked out over the plain to those baobab trees. I could just see the corner of the house of N'goma, the witchdoctor. Beyond it was a large mud-and-wattle dwelling of the Chief. The African followed my gaze.

'Bwana,' he said, 'it was called the village of rottenness by the mouths of many people and now I go to bring a new message. A school will be built and a church, Bwana. I will bring to them also the ways of health. The people of the village shall come to the hospital now. It will their Chief's order, and, Bwana, it will be I who will tell them about the Son of God, as well as the ways of health.'

Late that afternoon we watched him walk resolutely down the path of the hospital towards his own village. Simba was beside me.

'Bwana,' he said, 'truly you preached a strong sermon with those crocodile forceps of yours on the veranda here that afternoon. *Yah*, it's a sermon that M'bangho and the village of M'bovu will never forget.'

Look out for other Jungle Doctor titles in this series by Paul White

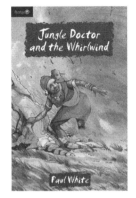

1
Jungle Doctor and the Whirlwind
ISBN 978-1-84550-296-6

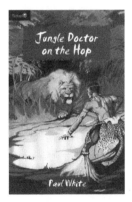

2
Jungle Doctor on the Hop
ISBN 978-1-84550-297-3

3
Jungle Doctor Spots a Leopard
ISBN 978-1-84550-301-7

4

Jungle Doctor's Crooked
Dealings
ISBN 978-1-84550-299-7

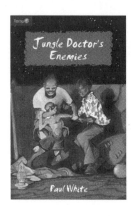

5

Jungle Doctor's Enemies
ISBN 978-1-84550-300-0

6

Jungle Doctor in Slippery Places
ISBN 978-1-84550-298-0

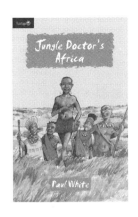

7

Jungle Doctor's Africa

ISBN 978-1-84550-388-8

8

Jungle Doctor on Safari

ISBN 978-1-84550-391-8

9

Jungle Doctor Meets a Lion

ISBN 978-1-84550-392-5

10

Eyes on Jungle Doctor

ISBN 978-1-84550-393-2

11

Jungle Doctor Stings a Scorpion

ISBN 978-1-84550-390-1

12

Jungle Doctor Pulls a Leg

ISBN 978-1-84550-389-5

CHRISTIAN FOCUS PUBLICATIONS

Christian Focus Christian Heritage CF4K Mentor

Christian Focus Publications publishes books for adults and children under its four main imprints: Christian Focus, CF4K, Mentor and Christian Heritage. Our books reflect that God's word is reliable and Jesus is the way to know him, and live for ever with him.

Our children's publication list includes a Sunday School curriculum that covers pre-school to early teens; puzzle and activity books. We also publish personal and family devotional titles, biographies and inspirational stories that children will love.

If you are looking for quality Bible teaching for children then we have an excellent range of Bible story and age specific theological books.

From pre-school to teenage fiction, we have it covered!

Find us at our web page:
www.christianfocus.com